The Clermont Book of
Backgammon

For my daughter Michel

The Clermont Book of Backgammon

by David Dor-El

WINCHESTER PRESS

Copyright © 1975 by David Dor-El

All rights reserved

Library of Congress Cataloging in Publication Data

Dor-El, David.
   The Clermont book of backgammon.

   1. Backgammon.   I. Title.
GV1469.B2D67   1979   795′.1   79-9728
ISBN 0-87691-298-6   0-87691-307-9 (paper)

The name "Clermont," and the Clermont Club logo ℭ on the front cover,
are used with the permission of the copyright and trademark owners.
The Clermont Club Limited ® 1962

WINCHESTER is a Trademark of Olin Corporation used by Winchester Press, Inc.
under authority and control of the Trademark Proprietor

Published by Winchester Press
1421 South Sheridan
Tulsa, Oklahoma 74114

Printed in the United States of America

First published in Great Britain by Queen Anne Press Limited

Diagrams by Typo Arts Limited
Cover design by David Fordham
Cover photography by Bob Marchant

2 3 4 5 6 7 8 9 — 85 84 83 82 81 80

Contents

Acknowledgements

I am deeply grateful to all the members of staff at the Clermont Club, London, and the Playboy Clubs in London and Manchester – directors, managers, and senior and junior staff – for their help day after day. At the same time I would like to take this opportunity of thanking all the members of those clubs, whom, I hope, have benefited from my classes or private lessons.

I would also like to thank Kirsty Nicholson of Queen Anne Press for looking after this book, and lastly Judy D., who for the last two years has been encouraging me to write it!

D. D-E

Foreword

The author has asked me to write this foreword for reasons that must have more to do with the fact that he works for me than because I am any kind of a backgammon player. Oh, I do know how to play the game, but I have long ago given up any pretensions to expertise.

During the trouble in Cyprus during 1974, I asked Yani Zagrophos, one of the Clermont Club members, what sort of a man Archbishop Makarios was. I knew Yani was personally acquainted with him. Yani deliberated for a moment, then he said very solemnly: 'He's a really terrible backgammon player.' To any serious backgammon player that answer would seem entirely appropriate. After all, if a man doesn't play backgammon properly, what possible saving grace could he possess that would warrant even the slightest consideration?

I think that to become a backgammon expert requires more concentration, more patience and more dedication than I am willing to devote to anything which people will always describe as 'only a game, after all'. Experts have to live with that deprecation of their obsession or challenge it. Obviously, a man who describes the spiritual and political leader of a whole country as 'a really terrible backgammon player' has decided to challenge the concept that it is 'only a game'. To the really expert backgammon player it isn't 'only a game'. It's the very quintessence of life. It's very much the way chess masters think of chess.

But backgammon has a little deceptive wrinkle that makes it more exciting than chess – at least to the beginner – and that's the element of chance, the luck of the dice. Alas, experience tells us that in the long run the luck factor evens out and the truly skilled player will prevail. You can get lucky and win from Barclay Cooke or any other expert today, but by the end of the week the expert will have gobbled you up. Beware!

What is it that the expert knows and you don't? He knows the percentages, *all* the percentages, and, as he glances at the dice and the various positions on the table, he calculates all the possibilities. He thinks what you are likely to throw on your next roll, and what the consequences will be depending on how he plays this move; and he mentally calculates the effects of his probable next roll. You don't play like that, and you probably never will, and even if you do you will then have to master the expert's sense of timing which tells him when to hurry up or when to slow down his progress, when to hit or when to be hit.

As I mentioned at the beginning, I have neither the patience nor the persistence ever to become a great backgammon player. But I have made two important contributions to the game. The first is that I taught Hugh Hefner the fundamentals of backgammon and he has become a first-class player who has done a great deal to popularise it in America. My other contribution was to employ David Dor-El to teach the game at the Clermont Club in London. I knew he understood mathematics (he taught the subject in a private school) and I believed this would be a great asset to anyone trying to teach the subtleties of the game. David's enormous success has proved me right.

You may decide, like me, to accept backgammon as 'just a game' and let the experts get on with their obsession. But if you don't decide this – or even if you do – you will gain some insight into the way the 'big boys' think from this book. For David Dor-El understands the mathematics of the game and can explain them in such a way that even people with an abhorrence of simple arithmetic will comprehend.

VICTOR LOWNES
London 1975

Introduction

On 24 March 1940 Sir Winston Churchill, the First Lord of the Admiralty, wrote to the Fourth Sea Lord:

'Backgammon would be a good game for Wardroom, Gunroom, and Warrant Officers' Mess, and I have no doubt it would amuse the sailors.

'Backgammon is a better game than cards for the circumstances of war-time afloat, because it whiles away twenty minutes or a quarter of an hour, whereas cards are a much longer business.'

Whether or not the Fourth Sea Lord then introduced the game to the Wardrooms, Gunrooms, and Warrant Officers' Messes I do not know; but this game – backgammon in English, Tric-Trac in French, Sheish-besh in the Middle East, name any country and they quite likely have, or had, some form of and name for the game – has been around for nearly five thousand years. It originated in the Middle East, at Ur in Mesopotamia and has survived the centuries despite being banned by the Romans and the Church. It still 'hooks' people today all over the world as it did in those early days.

Backgammon is a game of 'war' – of hitting your opponent's men. That's why it is a game of skill (like chess) and yet, it is also a racing game, as dice are used, and this gives it an element of luck. These two components, skill and luck, dominate the game; and it is the balance between them that gives it its fascination. It is a social game that appeals to all types of people. Men, women and children can play. Because it is fast, it is exciting and entertaining, and you can play for hours without getting tired or bored: but equally if you have only half an hour to spare, you can still play a couple of games. An expert can be beaten by a novice, and very often it is impossible to tell until the very last moment who is going to win.

Backgammon is extremely easy to learn and the basic moves are very simple. But playing to win? That's a different matter! It can be much more complicated than it may at first appear. During a game one may think one is going to win (due to one's great 'skill') but, with one's own hand, by rolling the dice, everything may suddenly be ruined – 'bad luck', of course.

Backgammon entered a new era about fifty years ago, when an unknown player in the United States invented the use of the doubling cube. And with this, skill in fact obtained a new dimension: new horizons were opened up and the game reached a turning point.

The object of this book is to supply you with the knowledge needed to master the game. That's why each chapter is complete in itself, and yet together they form a unique approach and will show you that backgammon is not just 'another game' after all!

I

Mathematical Information

The object of this chapter is to incorporate in one place all the mathematical information needed to play backgammon. Some sections will be applicable at any stage of the game, while others will apply only to a specific stage or situation.

With all the mathematical information embraced in one chapter, the remaining chapters will then be mainly devoted to the strategy and actual method of play.

SECTION ONE: COMBINATION OF THE DICE

TABLE 1: THE OUTCOME OF ROLLING TWO DICE

		DIE II					
		1	**2**	**3**	**4**	**5**	**6**
	1	1–1	1–2	1–3	1–4	1–5	1–6
	2	2–1	2–2	2–3	2–4	2–5	2–6
	3	3–1	3–2	3–3	3–4	3–5	3–6
DIE I	**4**	4–1	4–2	4–3	4–4	4–5	4–6
	5	5–1	5–2	5–3	5–4	5–5	5–6
	6	6–1	6–2	6–3	6–4	6–5	6–6

We know that each player alternately rolls two dice. On each die there are six different numbers, from 1 to 6. Imagine that one die is red, the other black. Now we can roll, for example, a 1 with the red die and a 1 with the black die; or, 3 with the red die and 5 with the black; or, 5 with the red die and 3 with the black. We can therefore have two different results when rolling the dice: either the numbers on each die may be different, e.g. 5 and 3, 4 and 2 – called the 'regular roll'; or the numbers on each die may be the same, e.g. 1 and 1, 2 and 2 – called the 'double roll'. Each regular roll is counted as two different combinations of the dice, i.e. 5 (red) and 3 (black) or 3 (red) and 5 (black). Both combinations must be included, so whenever you roll different numbers on the dice, it counts as two different combinations (see Table 1). A double roll can only produce one combination as the numbers are the same on each die. Thus there are six double rolls:

6–6	4–4	2–2
5–5	3–3	1–1

and thirty regular rolls:

6–5 or 5–6	5–4 or 4–5	4–2 or 2–4
6–4 or 4–6	5–3 or 3–5	4–1 or 1–4
6–3 or 3–6	5–2 or 2–5	3–2 or 2–3
6–2 or 2–6	5–1 or 1–5	3–1 or 1–3
6–1 or 1–6	4–3 or 3–4	2–1 or 1–2

So the total number of combinations obtainable from rolling two dice is thirty six – no more and no less. *(Note: Throughout the book the notation ( ) × is used to indicate the two different combinations of the dice in a regular roll, e.g. (6–5) × means 6–5 and 5–6.)*

Conclusions
1. The odds against throwing any double roll are 5 to 1.
2. The odds against throwing any specific double roll (e.g. 1–1) are 35 to 1.
3. The odds on throwing any regular roll are 5 to 1 in favour.
4. The odds against throwing any specific regular roll (e.g. 5–3) are 34 to 2 or, reduced to the lowest common denominator, 17 to 1.

SECTION TWO: THE PROBABILITY OF HITTING A BLOT

Now that you know all the possible combinations of the two dice you are in a position to calculate the probabilities of hitting a blot, or of having your blot hit by an opponent.

Assume that your opponent has left a blot and that only a 1 will be good to hit it – what chance do you actually have of hitting? We need a 1 so we need to know which combinations of the dice will show a 1, and how many there are. Well:

1–2 or 2–1	1–4 or 4–1	1–6 or 6–1
1–3 or 3–1	1–5 or 5–1	1–1

representing a total of 11 shots out of 36. (See Table 2, column a). So your chances of hitting the blot are approximately 2 to 1 against (see Table 3, first line).

Let's take another example. Your opponent has left a blot and you need a 6 to hit it. Let's see how many rolls in 36 will give you the required 6 (see Table 2, column b):

6–1 or 1–6	6–3 or 3–6	6–5 or 5–6
6–2 or 2–6	6–4 or 4–6	6–6

again, this is 11 out of 36. But if you roll 5–1, it too will give you a hit (5+ 1 = 6). So there are more than 11 shots:

5–1 or 1–5	(5+ 1 = 6)	2–2	(2+ 2+ 2 = 6)
4–2 or 2–4	(4+ 2 = 6)	3–3	(3+ 3 = 6)

That brings us to a total of 17 out of 36. So your chances of hitting the blot are almost even (1 to 1). (See Table 3, line 6). *However this only applies if your opponent is not holding an intervening point.* Studying Table 3, it is obvious that if a blot must be left exposed to a direct shot (that is, a distance of 1 to 6 spaces away, inclusive) the closer the blot is to the opponent's man the fewer are the chances of being hit. If the blot has to be exposed to a long shot (a distance of more than 6 spaces), the further away it is the better. Table 3 shows all the odds in your favour or against you.

A close study of Tables 2 and 3 is vital if you want to calculate the chances of being hit, and eliminate them. You will also have a much better understanding of the opening moves discussed in the next chapter.

TABLE 2: THE DIFFERENT WAYS IN WHICH EACH COMBINATION OF THE DICE CAN BE USED

COMBINATION OF THE DICE	a 1	2	3	4	5	b 6	7	8	9	10	11	12	15	16	18	20	24
1–1	○	○	●	●													
2–2		○		○		●		●									
3–3			○			○			●			●					
4–4				○				○				●		●			
5–5					○					○			●			●	
6–6						○						○			●		●
1–2	○	○	●														
2–1	○	○	●														
1–3	○		○	●													
3–1	○		○	●													
1–4	○			○	●												
4–1	○			○	●												
1–5	○				○	●											
5–1	○				○	●											
1–6	○					○	●										
6–1	○					○	●										
2–3		○	○		●												
3–2		○	○		●												
2–4		○		○		●											
4–2		○		○		●											
2–5		○			○		●										
5–2		○			○		●										
2–6		○				○		●									
6–2		○				○		●									
3–4			○	○			●										
4–3			○	○			●										
3–5			○		○			●									
5–3			○		○			●									
3–6			○			○			●								
6–3			○			○			●								
4–5				○	○				●								
5–4				○	○				●								
4–6				○		○				●							
6–4				○		○				●							
5–6					○	○					●						
6–5					○	○					●						
Total out of 36	11	12	14	15	15	17	6	6	5	3	2	3	1	1	1	1	1

Note: Each double roll can be used in four different ways, for example 2–2 can be used to move a distance of 2, 4, 6, or 8 spaces.

Each regular roll can be used in three different ways, 6–1 for example may be used to move a 1, 6, or 7 (6+1).

TABLE 3: THE PROBABILITY OF HITTING A BLOT

		OUT OF 36		Odds against being hit	% Chance of being hit
		Shots in your favour	Shots against you		
The distance between your opponent's blot and one of your men (no intervening closed points held by opponent).	1	11	25	25:11	~ 31%
	2	12	24	2:1	33%
	3	14	22	11:7	~ 39%
	4	15	21	7:5	~ 42%
	5	15	21	7:5	~ 42%
	6	17	19	19:17	47%
	7	6	30	5:1	~ 17%
	8	6	30	5:1	~ 17%
	9	5	31	6.2:1	14%
	10	3	33	11:1	8%
	11	2	34	17:1	~ 6%
	12	3	33	11:1	8%
	15	1	35	35:1	~ 3%
	16	1	35	35:1	~ 3%
	18	1	35	35:1	~ 3%
	20	1	35	35:1	~ 3%
	24	1	35	35:1	~ 3%

(~ = approximately)

SECTION THREE: THE PROBABILITY OF BEARING OFF THE LAST MAN IN ONE ROLL

In this section you can see the probability of bearing off the last man in one roll. In each case the location of the last man is given, together with the number of points needed to end the game, the number of shots out of 36 that you have for ending the game, the number of shots against you, the odds for and against you, and the probability of ending the game in the second roll should you not be able to bear off in the first.

TABLE 4: PROBABILITY OF BEARING OFF THE LAST MAN IN ONE ROLL

Location of last man	Total points left to end the game	No of shots out of 36 in your favour	No of shots out of 36 against you	Odds in your favour	Odds against you	Ending the game in second roll?
on point 1	1	36	=	—	=	=
on point 2	2	36	=	—	=	=
on point 3	3	36	=	—	=	=

Location of last man	Total points left to end the game	No of shots out of 36 in your favour	No of shots out of 36 against you	Odds in your favour	Odds against you	Ending the game in second roll?
on point 4	4	34	(2–1) × ↑ 2	17:1	—	YES
on point 5	5	31	(3–1) × (2–1) × (1–1) ↑ 5	6:1	—	YES
on point 6	6	27	(4–1) × (3–2) × (3–1) × (2–1) × (1–1) ↑ 9	3:1	—	YES

SECTION FOUR: THE PROBABILITY OF BEARING OFF THE LAST TWO MEN IN ONE ROLL

In this section we look at the probability of being able to bear off your last two men in one roll. Again, in each case the location of the men is given, as well as the points needed to end the game, the shots for and against you out of 36, the odds, and the probabilities of finishing the game in the second roll. This section is worth close study, for it will be very useful to you later on.

TABLE 5: PROBABILITY OF BEARING OFF THE LAST TWO MEN IN ONE ROLL

Location of last two men	Total points left to end the game	No of shots out of 36 in your favour	No of shots out of 36 against you	Odds in your favour	Odds against you	Ending the game in second roll?
on point 1	2	36	=	—	=	=
on points 1 and 2	3	36	=	—	=	=

Location of last two men	Total points left to end the game	No of shots out of 36 in your favour	No of shots out of 36 against you	Odds in your favour	Odds against you	Ending the game in second roll?
on points 1 and 3	4	34	$(2-1) \times$ ↑ 2	17:1	—	YES
on points 1 and 4	5	29	$(3-2) \times$ $(3-1) \times$ $(2-1) \times$ $(1-1)$ ↑ 7	4:1	—	YES
on point 2	4	26	$(6-1) \times$ $(5-1) \times$ $(4-1) \times$ $(3-1) \times$ $(2-1) \times$ ↑ 10	2.6:1	—	YES
on points 2 and 3	5	25	$(6-1) \times$ $(5-1) \times$ $(4-1) \times$ $(3-1) \times$ $(2-1) \times$ $(1-1)$ ↑ 11	2.2:1	—	YES
on points 1 and 5	6	23	$(4-3) \times$ $(4-2) \times$ $(4-1) \times$ $(3-2) \times$ $(3-1) \times$ $(2-1) \times$ $(1-1)$ ↑ 13	1.7:1	—	YES
on points 2 and 4	6	23	$(6-1) \times$ $(5-1) \times$ $(4-1) \times$ $(3-2) \times$ $(3-1) \times$ $(2-1) \times$ $(1-1)$ ↑ 13	1.7;1	—	YES

Location of last two men	Total points left to end the game	No of shots out of 36 in your favour	No of shots out of 36 against you	Odds in your favour	Odds against you	Ending the game in second roll?
on point 3	6	17	(6–2) × (6–1) × (5–2) × (5–1) × (4–2) × (4–1) × (3–2) × (3–1) × (2–1) × (1–1) ↑ 19	—	1:1	YES
on points 2 and 5	7	19	(6–1) × (5–1) × (4–3) × (4–2) × (4–1) × (3–2) × (3–1) × (2–1) × (1–1) ↑ 17	1:1	—	NO
on points 3 and 4	7	17	(6–2) × (6–1) × (5–2) × (5–1) × (4–2) × (4–1) × (3–2) × (3–1) × (2–1) × (1–1) ↑ 19	—	1:1	NO
on points 1 and 6	7	(6–5) × (6–4) × (6–3) × (6–2) × (6–1) × (2–2) (3–3) (4–4) (5–5) (6–6) ↑ 15	21	—	7:5	NO

Location of last two men	Total points left to end the game	No of shots out of 36 in your favour	No of shots out of 36 against you	Odds in your favour	Odds against you	Ending the game in second roll?
on points 3 and 5	8	(6–5) × (6–4) × (6–3) × (5–4) × (5–3) × (3–3) (4–4) (5–5) (6–6) ↑ 14	22	—	11:7	NO
on points 2 and 6	8	(6–5) × (6–4) × (6–3) × (6–2) × (2–2) (3–3) (4–4) (5–5) (6–6) ↑ 13	23	—	1:1.7	NO
on point 4	8	(6–5) × (6–4) × (5–4) × (2–2) (3–3) (4–4) (5–5) (6–6) ↑ 11	25	—	1:2.2	NO
on points 3 and 6	9	(6–5) × (6–4) × (6–3) × (3–3) (4–4) (5–5) (6–6) 10	26	—	1:2.6	NO

Location of last two men	Total points left to end the game	No of shots out of 36 in your favour	No of shots out of 36 against you	Odds in your favour	Odds against you	Ending the game in second roll?
on points 4 and 5	9	(6–5) × (6–4) × (5–4) × (3–3) (4–4) (5–5) (6–6) ↑ 10	26	—	1:2.6	NO
on points 4 and 6	10	(6–5) × (6–4) × (3–3) (4–4) (5–5) (6–6) ↑ 8	28	—	7:2	NO
on point 5	10	(6–5) × (3–3) (4–4) (5–5) (6–6) ↑ 6	30	—	5:1	NO
on points 5 and 6	11	(6–5) × (3–3) (4–4) (5–5) (6–6) ↑ 6	30	—	5:1	NO
on point 6	12	(3–3) (4–4) (5–5) (6–6) ↑ 4	32	—	8:1	NO

SECTION FIVE: THE PROBABILITY OF ENTERING ONE OR TWO MEN FROM THE BAR IN ONE ROLL

Table 6 below shows you the odds for and against you when you are trying to enter from the bar with one or two men. The formula for working this out is very simple; for instance, if you take N to represent the open points in your opponent's home board (or closed points belonging to you) and you have one man on the bar, the chances of your getting in in one roll are $(12 - N) \times N$. So, if $N = 3$, then $12 - 3 = 9$, and $9 \times 3 = 27$, thus you have 27 possible shots out of 36 which will enable you to enter, i.e. odds of 3 to 1 in your favour. If you have two men on the bar then the formula is simply N^2, N again representing the number of open points on your opponent's home board. So, if three points are open, then $3 \times 3 = 9$, so you have 9 shots out of 36 which will allow you to enter both men in one roll, i.e. odds of 3 to 1 against you. It is obviously important to be able to calculate at a glance your chances of entering from the bar when your opponent is building up his board and you are debating whether or not to take a risk and leave a blot.

TABLE 6: ENTERING FROM THE BAR

In one roll			$(12-N) \times N$		N^2			In one roll
One man only				N	Two men simultaneously			
% in your favour	Odds in your favour	No of ways against you	No of ways out of 36 in your favour	No of points open	No of ways out of 36 in your favour	No of ways against you	Odds in your favour	% in your favour
98%	35:1	1	35	5	25	11	25:11	69%
~89%	8:1	4	32	4	16	20		44%
75%	3:1	9	27	3	9	27		25%
~56%	5:4	16	20	2	4	32		11%
~31%	25:11	25	11	1	1	35		3%

(Odds here are against you)

INSTRUCTIONS FOR USING THIS TABLE
SAY No OF OPEN POINTS IN YOUR OPPONENT'S HOME BOARD IS $N = 3$

If you have one man on the bar, then,
  $(12-3) = 9$
  $9 \times 3 = 27$
You have 27 shots out of 36 which will bring in this man in one roll or 3 to 1 odds in your favour.

If you have two men on the bar, then,
  $N^2 = 3^2 = 9$
You have 9 shots out of 36 which will bring in the two men in one roll or 3 to 1 odds *against* you.

SECTION SIX: DIFFERENT SYSTEMS OF EVALUATING YOUR OWN AND YOUR OPPONENT'S POSITION

There are three ways to evaluate your own and your opponent's position during the game:
I. The number of points (pips) left to end the game.
  a) Addition
  b) Difference

II. The number of rolls left to end the game.
   a) Division
III. Strength of the tables.

I. Evaluating the position of the game by the number of pips needed to end the game

We want a numerical system that will enable us to calculate the position of each player and will tell us at any given moment of the game which of the two players is leading and by how much.

We are in fact using the system adopted when bearing off the last one or two men in one roll. In that case (see Table 5) we gave a man on point 1, 1 point – that is what he needed to end the game. A man on point 3 needed 3 points. In other words each man is evaluated according to the number of the point he lands on. So, a man on point 24 needs 24 points to finish the game. First he needs 18 points to get him home to our point 6, and then another 6 points to be taken off. So, using this system it can be seen that at the beginning of each game each player needs 167 points to get all his men home and off the board. This is calculated as follows:

Two men on point 24	2×24	48 points
Five men on point 13	5×13	65 points
Three men on point 8	3×8	24 points
Five men on point 6	5×6	30 points
	Total	167 points

So at the beginning of each game you know you need 167 points to finish the game. As the game progresses you may of course have some men put on the bar, and need more points – but 167 is the *least* number you need.

a) Addition
In order to determine who is leading at any stage of the game you can simply add up the total points of your men (according to the number of the point they are on as discussed) and then do the same for your opponent's men. The difference between the two totals will show you who is leading and by how much. Do not forget though when calculating your opponent's score that his 1-point is your 24-point and vice versa.

b) Difference
This is basically the same system as above, but it is much quicker since you do not count points for your men if your opponent has a man, or men, on the same point number. For instance, if player A has one man on point 6 and player B also has a man on his point 6, since both players need a 6 to bear their respective men off, the two cancel each other out and you need not count them. Similarly if player A has three men on his 13-point and player B has two men on his 13-point, then player A only has to account for his extra man, i.e. 13 points. (Player B evaluates his position in the same way.)

II. The number of rolls needed to end the game

A second way of working out the relative positions of the two players is according to the number of rolls each needs to finish the game. If we go back to the combinations of the dice, the total value of all the combinations, including doubles, adds up to 294. If we divide this by 36 (the number of different combinations) we arrive at a mean (average) of 8.16. Since we want to know how many rolls are left, the 0.16 has no value, so we round off the figure to 8. This means that we expect to have an average of 8 points on each roll; therefore we allot 8 points to one roll, 16 to two rolls, and so on.

a) Division

So, if you want to know who is leading in terms of rolls, you merely divide the difference between the two point counts (obtained by either method 1a or 1b) by 8 and you have the answer. For example, if you are leading by 24 points, divide by 8, and you can see that you lead by three rolls.

III. **Strength of the tables**

This is a quick method to check roughly who is leading in terms of rolls.

For each man in your outerboard you need one roll to bring it into your homeboard. For each man in your opponent's outerboard you need two rolls to bring it home, and for each man in your opponent's homeboard you need three rolls. Add up the number of rolls needed, and then do the same for your opponent's men. The difference between the two totals will give you the leader. Now let us look at some examples.

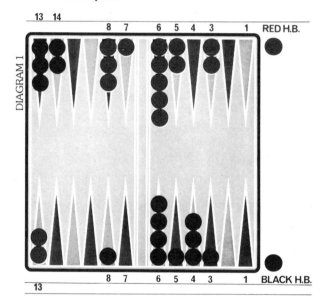

We want to find out who is leading in Diagram 1, so let's first calculate Black's position by the 'addition' method:

Now, let's see what the position is for Red.

One man on point 3	1×3	=	3		Two men on point 3	2×3	=	6
Three men on point 4	3×4	=	12		Two men on point 5	2×5	=	10
One man on point 5	1×5	=	5		Five men on point 6	5×6	=	30
Four men on point 6	4×6	=	24		One man on point 7	1×7	=	7
One man on point 8	1×8	=	8		Three men on point 8	3×8	=	24
Three men on point 13	3×13	=	39		Two men on point 13	2×13	=	26
Two men on point 14	2×14	=	28					103
			119					

Total number of points for Black = 119.

Total number of points for Red = 103, so Red is leading by $119 - 103 = 16$.

Now let's calculate the positions according to the differences – comparing the man (or men) on opposing symmetrical points. In other words, how many men do you have on your 3–point compared with the number your opponent has on his 3–point, and so on.

Red has:

One extra man on point 3	1×3	=	3
One extra man on point 5	1×5	=	5
One extra man on point 6	1×6	=	6
One man on point 7	1×7	=	7
Two extra men on point 8	2×8	=	16
			37

According to this calculation Red has 37 points.

Let's take a look now at Black's position, using the same method.

Three men on point 4	3×4	=	12
One extra man on point 13	1×13	=	13
Two men on point 14	2×14	=	28
			53

So Black has 53 points. The difference between the two is $53 - 37 = 16$: the same as before.

Now let's translate this lead in number of points into the lead in terms of rolls. Divide 16 by 8 (8 being the average roll as we saw previously) to give an answer of two rolls. Therefore we can say that Red is leading by two rolls.

Let's look at the positions using the third way discussed above, i.e. a rough check of the strength of the tables.

Red has:

Four men in his outerboard	4×1	=	4
Two men in his opponent's outerboard	2×2	=	4
			8

Therefore Red needs eight rolls to bring these six men into his homeboard.

Black has:

One man in his outerboard	1×1	=	1
Five men in his opponent's outerboard	5×2	=	10
			11

So Black needs eleven rolls to bring his six men into his homeboard. According to this system Red is leading by three rolls as opposed to the two rolls shown previously. But don't forget this is only a rough guide – we have not taken into consideration the men already in each player's homeboard. So be careful if you use this method, for it does not give a totally accurate figure. It is only a quick way of getting an approximate idea of who is leading. You must also remember to take into account who is the next to play. Red is leading by two rolls in Diagram 1 so if he is to play next then he will be three rolls ahead. However if it is Black to play then Red will be leading by only one roll.

SECTION SEVEN: WHEN TO RUN WITH YOUR LAST MAN

Knowing when to run with your last man is fundamental in backgammon. It will often save you from being gammoned, and is a crucial factor in the art of the back game.

First of all, you must be totally familiar with the board. So use it. Always have it out when you are reading this book, constantly practise on it, count on it, and thoroughly familiarize yourself with it. The more you do this, the easier you will find it to understand and master strategies that may, at first sight, appear to be very complex.

We are concerned now with your last man: to run or not to run? Well, let's assume that you have one man on your 24-point (your opponent's 1-point). You have been waiting for a shot at your opponent but, so far, it has not come. You roll double 6. Three 6s will take your man to your

6-point (24 − 18 = 6) and one more will bear that man off. So if with that roll you do move your man from the 24-point, you save yourself from being gammoned. Obviously you must run. However, if you roll a double 5 (your last man is again on your 24-point), this will only take you to your 4-point (24 − 20 = 4), and will not save you from being gammoned. If your last man is on point 23, and you roll double 6, you can move to point 5 (3 × 6 = 18; 23 − 18 = 5) and take a man off, thus saving the game. Double 5 will take you to point 3 (4 × 5 = 20; 23 − 20 = 3) but will not enable you to bear off a man − thus you still lose a gammon. Now move your man up to point 22. Double 6 will take you to point 4 and leave one 6 to be used for bearing off (22 − 18 = 4; one 6 left to play) hence saving you the game. Double 5 will take you from point 22 to point 2 (22 − 20 = 2) and double 4 will bring you to your point 6 (22 − 16 = 6). However neither double 5 nor 4 will help you save the game. Similarly you can work out your chances of saving the game from the other points. (These will be held mainly in your opponent's home-board, or − occasionally − in his outerboard.)

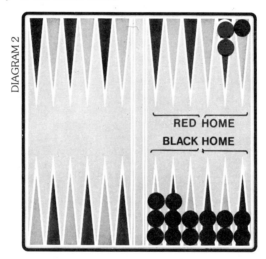

Now let's look at a more complicated situation, such as that shown in Diagram 2. Black has a roll with which he can either run and get near home (but not actually into his home) or stay, and move the men in his homeboard. Should he stay behind or run to try to save his game? If he stays it is because he is hoping that Red will roll any 1, thereby being forced to hit on the 1-point (excluding double 1, for then Red would automatically end the game). The chances that Red will roll any 1 − other than double 1 − are 10 out of 36 (10/36). Having been hit and put on the bar *Black* then has to roll any 1 − including doubles − in order to hit back and save the game. His chances are 11 out of 36 (11/36). Therefore the compound probability, the probability that these two events will happen in succession, is:

$$\frac{10}{36} \times \frac{11}{36} = \frac{110}{1296} \qquad \sim 1 \text{ to } 12$$

In other words Black's chances are 12 to 1 against saving the game if he stays and approximately 3 to 1 against saving it if he runs. Therefore he must run.

However, if Red should have three men left on his 2-point, then it's a different story. If Red rolls any 1 (excluding 1−1) Black will have 20 return shots because Red will have had no option but to leave two blots, one on point 1, and one on point 2, having hit Black and put him on the bar. The compound probability now looks like this:

$$\frac{10}{36} \times \frac{20}{36} = \frac{200}{1296} \qquad \sim 6 \text{ to } 1$$

Black's odds are approximately 6 to 1 against saving the game – double the chances he had before – so he must stay behind. This situation is known as 'the classic'.

What though if Red has four men left on his 2-point? Well, Red needs at least two rolls to end the game (unless of course he rolls one of five good doubles, 6–6, 5–5, 4–4, 3–3, 2–2), so if Black rolls a long shot then he must use it to run. If he doesn't roll one then he should stay, because any 1 (excluding double 1) will force Red to hit and thereby give Black a shot – and a chance to save the game. The same rules apply when Red has five men left on his 2-point. In fact the situation is slightly better for Black here as even a double throw will not enable Red to finish the game.

If you have two men on your opponent's 1-point, check before you run with one of them how many men your opponent has on his 2-point. You may be able to play in such a way as to arrive at 'the classic' position we discussed above.

SECTION EIGHT: WORKING OUT YOUR EXPECTATION OF THE GAME

Being able to work out your expectation of the game is another vitally important factor. Let's have a look at Diagram 3.

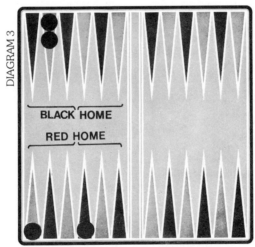

DIAGRAM 3

BLACK HOME

RED HOME

It is Black's turn to roll and he wants to know whether to double. Well, out of 36, he has 26 good shots that will finish the game for him in one roll (26/36). That leaves 10 out of 36 shots that are bad and which will give Red the chance of a roll – and a win. Red on the other hand has 29 shots out of 36 (29/36) that are good and 7 out of 36 (7/36) that will prove bad. Therefore, if Black does not double, his chances of winning the game are:

$$\left(\frac{26}{36}\right) + \left[\left(\frac{10}{36}\right) \times \left(\frac{7}{36}\right)\right] = \frac{1006}{1296}$$

Black's chances of not winning are:

$$1 - \left(\frac{1006}{1296}\right) = \frac{290}{1296}$$

Black's net expectation of winning is therefore:

$$\frac{1006}{1296} - \frac{290}{1296} = \frac{716}{1296} = 0.55 \text{ (of the original unit being played for)}$$

But if Black doubles – and now everything depends on his first roll, because he may not get the chance of a second roll if he is redoubled and has to concede – then his expectation is:

$$\left[\left(\frac{26}{36} \right) - \left(\frac{10}{36} \right) \right] \times 2^* = 0.88 \text{ (of the original agreed unit being played for)}$$

*Doubles to 2

Therefore Black must double. If you have a plus expectation on the last roll, you *must* double.

Now what about Red? Well, Black's chances are less than 3 to 1 so Red would obviously prefer not to be doubled but, once the double is offered, he has to accept.

Now you have the formula for working out your expectation of the game you can apply it whenever you are considering a double in the final stages of the game.

SECTION NINE: WORKING OUT SETTLEMENTS

A game of backgammon may be settled between the two players at any stage, i.e. without them finishing it. After all, there is no rule that states you must play to the bitter end! But, how do they come to a settlement and why do they agree to settle? To answer this we need to look at an example. (Diagram 4)

It is Black to roll. He has 15 shots out of 36 (15/36) in his favour, but if he rolls any one of the remaining 21 shots (21/36) he will lose. Suppose that both players come into this position 36 times. Black can expect to win 15 games and lose 21 games. In other words, his net expectation is:

$$\frac{15}{36} - \frac{21}{36} = \frac{15 - 21}{36} = \frac{-6}{36} = \frac{-1}{6}$$

So Black can expect to lose on the thirty-six games an average of one-sixth of the original unit (the stake agreed between the players at the beginning) per game. Now suppose the doubling cube is on 4. Black's expectation will now be:

$$\frac{-1}{6} \times 4 = \frac{-2}{3} \text{ of a unit}$$

Much depends of course on whose side the doubling cube is. To make this point a bit clearer let's look at a situation that occurred between two players, an Englishman and a South African, at the Clermont Club.

The game had reached the position shown in Diagram 5.

It is Red to roll. There are three different types of roll for him here:

1. He cannot move with 6–5, 5–5, 6–6   (4/36)
2. He can move but doesn't hit with 6–4 ×, 6–2 ×, 6–1 ×, 5–4 ×, 5–2 ×, 5–1 ×, 4–2 ×, 4–1 ×, 2–1 ×, 1–1, 2–2, 4–4   (21/36)
3. He can move and hit at the same time with 6–3 ×, 5–3 ×, 4–3 ×, 3–2 ×, 3–1 ×, 3–3   (11/36)

Assuming that only the rolls in the last category make him a favourite to win (while all the other rolls favour Black), then Red's expectation is:

$$\left[\left(\frac{11}{36} \right) - \left(\frac{25}{36} \right) \right] \times 32^* = -12.44 = \sim -12$$

*Cube is on 32 on Red's side

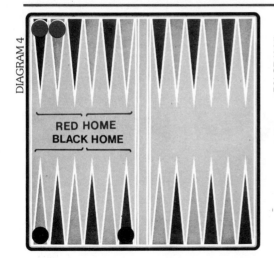

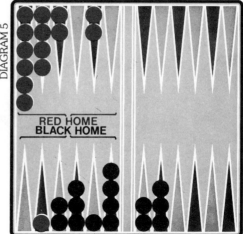

It would not be unfair for Red to give 12 points in settlement; but because he controls the doubling cube he has some bargaining power and the game was eventually settled with Red only giving 8 points to Black. This is a good example of the power that can be exerted when one has control of the doubling cube!

When working out a settlement always check the different rolls for you and your opponent – the good rolls, the bad ones, and the neutral ones. Then calculate your expectation as above – and, most important, take into account which side the cube is on. This is the factor that will finally influence the settlement and is the reason why the actual settlement will differ from the mathematical figure.

II

The Opening Move

The object of this chapter is to give you all the mathematical information you may need about each opening move, and to what you may commit yourself by choosing to play one particular move rather than another. When actually to play a specific opening move is another matter, and information on this is given in Chapter VIII. I have also given some special suggestions for beginners in the Appendix, 'Backgammon for Beginners'.

First of all, try to remember that from the point of view of probabilities there are, in backgammon, three different types. First there is the *absolute probability*. For example, if you want to hit a blot that is 10 pips away from your nearest man then you can use either 6–4, or 4–6, or 5–5, provided that your opponent has no closed points in the intervening space. If he does hold a point, as in the example in Diagram 12, then Red cannot use the roll 5–5 to run with one of his back men and hit Black's blot on the 11-point because 5s are being blocked by the Black men on Black's 6-point. This therefore reduces the absolute probability from 11 to 1 (3 out of 36) to 17 to 1 (2 out of 36) against hitting. The absolute probability has thus become the *rational probability* or the *gammon probability*.

The third type of probability is the *inconvenient probability*. If we look at the situation in Diagram 11 and assume that Red has rolled 3–3, we can see that he can hit Black's blot in the outerboard; but it would be much better for Red to use this roll in a different way rather than indulge in hitting just for the sheer enjoyment of it! (For the correct move here see Chapter III, The Response to the Opening Move.) In this chapter I am mainly concerned with the first two probabilities, the absolute and the gammon. As far as the third, the inconvenient probability, is concerned you will I think find it helpful to work out for yourself all the possible combinations that could give you a hit but might be better employed elsewhere. This exercise will give you a greater familiarity with the opening moves and hence a deeper understanding of them.

I would now like to clarify another point. Let's go back to Diagram 11. It states there that Red may, with one of his back men, use 5–4 or 4–5 to hit the Black blot. The 4–5 is straightforward. Red moves the 4 first and then the 5 and hits. But what about the 5–4? After all, Red cannot move 5 with his back man, so why do we still take this throw into consideration? Well, if we rolled one die first, moving the number shown (say 5), then rolled the second die and moved that (say 4) then obviously Red would not be able to use 5–4 to hit. However in backgammon we roll both dice together, so Red will be able to use 5–4 to hit, by moving the 4 first.

Each of the following diagrams will show the position after the appropriate opening move has been made, with arrows indicating from where the man or men have moved. Remember you are always moving *from* your point 24 *towards* your point 1; so it doesn't matter which side of the bar the homeboards are. More important, counting from 24 to 1 simplifies your moves and gives you an easy check. For instance, in Diagram 15 we have the opening move 6–5. Black moves one of his back men from point 24 to point 13, $24 - 13 = 11$, and 11 is the sum of the roll 6–5.

I have divided the opening moves into six different categories:

1. *Moves that make a point* (PM)
This group contains all the moves that enable you to make a point – either your bar-point or in your homeboard.

2. *Building Moves* (BM)
These are the moves in which you bring up builders hoping to be able to make a point on your next move provided of course that the builders are not hit. For then you must first enter from the bar before looking to see whether or not you can make a point.

3. *Running Moves* (RM)
In this group are the opening moves that will enable you to run with one of your back men.

4. *Building-Running Moves* (B-RM)
These moves are the ones that combine running with one of your back men and building in your outerboard, in the hope of making a point next time (again provided your builders are not hit).

5. *Chance Moves* (CM)
These are moves which, by taking a deliberate chance, will either help you to better your position next time or will give your opponent an opportunity to hit you *only* at the expense of what would otherwise be a good roll for him.

6. *Building-Chance Moves* (B-CM)
These moves all contain a high risk element and mainly commit you to back game strategy. Judge them for yourself and be sure you know how to play against them if you see your opponent using them!

There is a seventh category of opening move – the full run move, i.e. running with both back men. This is very popular in the Middle East where they are not familiar with the doubling cube, but since the cube plays an important part in our game I have not included full run moves in this book.

1. MOVES THAT ENABLE YOU TO MAKE A POINT (PM)
THE ROLL: 3–1 (Diagram 6)
With this roll you make the strongest point in your homeboard; this move may lead to a blocking strategy.

THE ROLL: 6–1 (Diagram 7)
Here you make your bar-point, producing half a prime; this may lead to a blocking strategy.

THE ROLL: 4–2 (Diagram 8)
This roll enables you to make the second most important point in your homeboard. It too may lead to a blocking strategy.

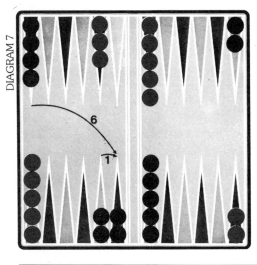

DIAGRAM 6

THE ROLL: 3–1

THE MOVE: 8→5, 6→5
TYPE OF MOVE: P.M.

No of blots left: —
No of ways to hit those blots: —
No of ways of not hitting those blots: —
Odds in your favour: —
Odds against you: —
% in your favour: —
% against you: —

Recommended (for beginners as well)

DIAGRAM 7

THE ROLL: 6–1

THE MOVE: 13→7, 8→7
TYPE OF MOVE: P.M.

No of blots left: —
No of ways to hit those blots: —
No of ways of not hitting those blots: —
Odds in your favour: —
Odds against you: —
% in your favour: —
% against you: —

Recommended (for beginners as well)

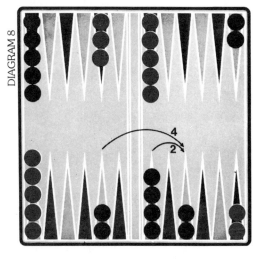

DIAGRAM 8

THE ROLL: 4–2

THE MOVE: 8→4, 6→4
TYPE OF MOVE: P.M.

No of blots left: —
No of ways to hit those blots: —
No of ways of not hitting those blots: —
Odds in your favour: —
Odds against you: —
% in your favour: —
% against you: —

Recommended (for beginners as well)

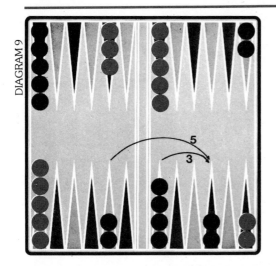

DIAGRAM 9

THE ROLL: 5–3

THE MOVE: 8→3, 6→3
TYPE OF MOVE: P.M.

No of blots left: —
No of ways to hit those blots: —
No of ways of not hitting those blots: —
Odds in your favour: —
Odds against you: —
% in your favour: —
% against you: —

Recommended (for beginners as well)

THE ROLL: 5–3 (Diagram 9)
With this roll you can make a low point in your homeboard, which may help you to slow the advance of your opponent's back men.

2. BUILDING MOVES (BM)
THE ROLL: 5–4 (Diagram 10)
If Black's blot is not hit he may use it next time round to make either his 5-point with 4–3 ×, 4–1 ×, 4–4 (5/36 chances) or his bar-point with 6–2 ×, 2–1 ×, 2–2 (5/36 chances) – a total of 10 out of 36 chances! Red of course may respond by making either point should he roll 4–4 or 6–6. This move may lead to a blocking strategy.

THE ROLL: 5–3 (Diagram 11)
If Black's blot is not hit he may use it to make his 5-point with 5–3 ×, 5–1 ×, (4/36 chances) or, failing that, his bar-point with 6–3 ×, 3–1 × (if Red has blocked the 5-point with 4–4 he cannot use this roll in its 'classical' manner), or 3–3 (5/36 chances), giving a total of 9 out of 36 chances. This move may lead to a blocking game strategy.

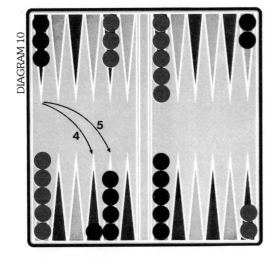

DIAGRAM 10

THE ROLL: 5–4

THE MOVE: 13→8, 13→9
TYPE OF MOVE: B.M.

No of blots left: 1
No of ways to hit those blots: 6. (6–2) × ; (5–3) × ;
   (4–4); (2–2)
No of ways of not hitting those blots: 30
Odds in your favour: 5 to 1 against being hit
Odds against you: —
% in your favour: —
% against you: —

Recommended (for beginners as well)

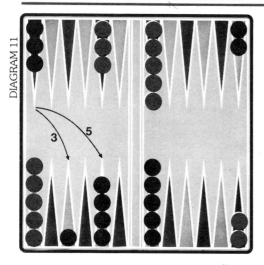

DIAGRAM 11

THE ROLL: 5–3

THE MOVE: 13 →8, 13 →10
TYPE OF MOVE: B.M.

No of blots left: 1
No of ways to hit those blots: 5. (6–3) × ; (5–4) × ;
  (3–3)
No of ways of not hitting those blots: 31
Odds in your favour: ~ 6 to 1 against being hit
Odds against you: —
% in your favour: —
% against you: —

Recommended

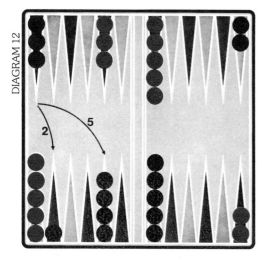

DIAGRAM 12

THE ROLL: 5–2

THE MOVE: 13 → 8, 13 → 11
TYPE OF MOVE: B.M.

No of blots left: 1
No of ways to hit those blots: 2. (6–4) ×
No of ways of not hitting those blots: 34
Odds in your favour: 17 to 1 against being hit
Odds against you: —
% in your favour: —
% against you: —

Recommended (for beginners as well)

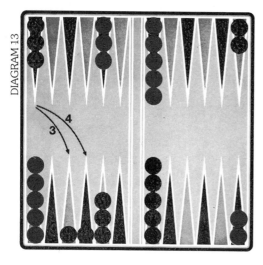

DIAGRAM 13

THE ROLL: 4–3

THE MOVE: 13 → 9, 13 → 10
TYPE OF MOVE: —

No of blots left: 2
No of ways to hit those blots: 11. (6–2) × ; (5–3) × ;
  (4–4); (2–2); (6–3) × ; (5–4) × ; (3–3)
No of ways of not hitting those blots: 25
Odds in your favour: ~ 2 to 1 against being hit
Odds against you: —
% in your favour: —
% against you: —

Recommended (for beginners as well)

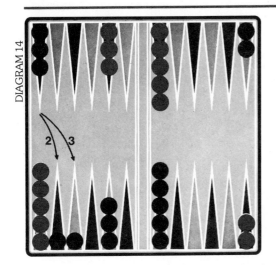

DIAGRAM 14

THE ROLL: 3–2

THE MOVE: 13→10, 13→11
TYPE OF MOVE: B.M.

No of blots left: 2
No of ways to hit those blots: 7. (6–3) × ; (5–4) × ;
   (3–3); (6–4) ×
No of ways of not hitting those blots: 29
Odds in your favour: ~ 4 to 1 against being hit
Odds against you: —
% in your favour: —
% against you: —

Recommended (for beginners as well)

THE ROLL: 5–2 (Diagram 12)
If Black's blot is not hit he may use it to make either his 5-point with 6–3 ×, 6–1 × (note, he does *not* use this roll to make the bar-point if he can make the 5-point) or 3–3 (5/36 chances) or his bar-point with 6–4 ×, 4–1 × (4/36 chances) – a total of 9 out of 36 chances. This move may lead to a blocking game strategy.

THE ROLL: 4–3 (Diagram 13)
If neither of Black's blots are hit he may use either one or both of them to make his 5-point with 5–4 ×, 5–3 ×, 5–1 ×, 4–3 ×, 4–1 ×, 4–4 (11/36 chances) or his bar-point with 6–3 ×, 6–2 ×, 3–1 × (he will only use this to make the bar-point if the 5-point has been blocked by Red), 2–1 ×, 2–2, 3–3 (9/36 chances) – a total of 20 chances out of 36. This move may lead to a very strong blocking game strategy.

THE ROLL: 3–2 (Diagram 14)
If Black's two blots escape being hit he may use them to make either his 5-point with 6–5 ×, 6–3 ×, 6–1 × (*not* making the bar-point) 5–3 ×, 5–1 ×, 3–3 (11/36 chances) or his bar-point with 6–4 ×, 6–3 ×, 4–3 ×, 4–1 ×, 3–1 × (if he cannot use this to block the 5-point) (10/36 chances), giving a total not of 21 but 19 chances out of 36 because 6–3 × was included twice. This is a move that may lead to a very strong blocking game strategy.

3. RUNNING MOVES (RM)
THE ROLL: 6–5 (Diagram 15)
This move allows you to escape with one of your back men to safety. You are not really worried about leaving one man behind as even if Red does roll a number enabling him to hit, he might prefer to use it elsewhere (remember the inconvenient probability?). Only double 5 would be painful because then Red will make two points in his homeboard hitting you at the same time – but then the chances of double 5 are 35 to 1 against. This move may lead to a running game strategy.

THE ROLL: 6–4 (Diagram 16)
With this move you start with one of your back men but you must remember that you may be hit twice. (Red may use the roll 5–2 × to this end.) The move may lead to a running game strategy, or to a back game strategy should you be twice hit.

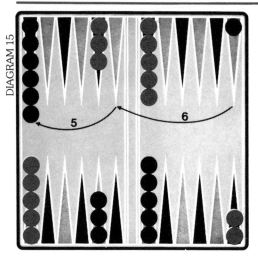

DIAGRAM 15

THE ROLL: 6–5

THE MOVE: 24 → 13
TYPE OF MOVE: R.M.

No of blots left: 1
No of ways to hit those blots: 22. (6–5) × ; (6–1) × ;
    (5–4) × ; (5–3) × ; (5–2) × ; (5–1) × ; (4–3) × ;
    (4–1) × ; (3–2) × ; (3–3); (4–4); (5–5); (6–6)
No of ways of not hitting those blots: 14
Odds in your favour: —
Odds against you: 11 to 7 being hit
% in your favour: —
% against you: —

Recommended (for beginners as well)

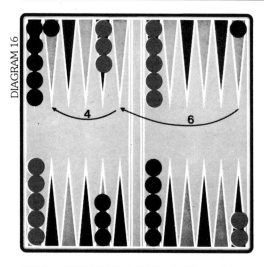

DIAGRAM 16

THE ROLL: 6–4

THE MOVE: 24 → 14
TYPE OF MOVE: R.M.

No of blots left: 2
No of ways to hit those blots: 27. (6–5) × ; (6–1) × ;
    (5–4) × ; (5–3) × ; (5–2) × ; (5–1) × ; (4–3) × ;
    (4–1) × ; (3–2) × ; (3–3); (4–4); (5–5); (6–6);
    (6–2) × ; (4–2) × ; (2–1) × ; (2–2)
No of ways of not hitting those blots: 9
Odds in your favour: —
Odds against you: 3 to 1 being hit once
% in your favour: —
% against you: —

Recommended (for beginners as well)

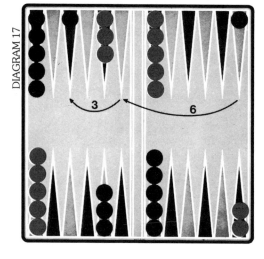

DIAGRAM 17

THE ROLL: 6–3

THE MOVE: 24 → 15
TYPE OF MOVE: R.M.

No of blots left: 2
No of ways to hit those blots: 26. (6–5) × ; (6–1) × ;
    (5–4) × ; (5–3) × ; (5–1) × ; (4–3) × ; (4–1) × ;
    (3–2) × ; (3–3); (4–4); (5–5); (6–6); (6–3) × ;
    (3–1) × ; (2–1) ×
No of ways of not hitting those blots: 10
Odds in your favour: —
Odds against you: 13 to 5 being hit once
% in your favour: —
% against you: —

Recommended (for beginners as well)

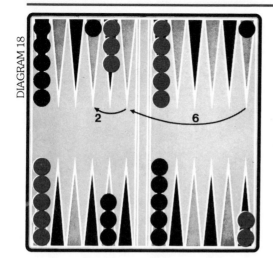

DIAGRAM 18

THE ROLL: 6–2

THE MOVE: 24 → 16
TYPE OF MOVE: R.M.

No of blots left: 2
No of ways to hit those blots: 27. (6–5) × ; (6–1) × ;
  (5–4) × ; (5–3) × ; (5–2) × ; (5–1) × ; (4–3) × ;
  (4–1) × ; (3–2) × ; (3–3); (4–4); (5–5); (6–6);
  (6–4) × ; (4–2) × ; (3–1) × ; (2–2)
No of ways of not hitting those blots: 9
Odds in your favour: —
Odds against you: 3 to 1 being hit once
% in your favour: —
% against you: —

Recommended (for beginners as well)

THE ROLL: 6–3   (Diagram 17)
The principle here is the same as in the previous roll. You can start to move with one of your back men taking into consideration that Red may hit twice if he should roll 5–3 × . The move can lead either to a running game strategy or, if hit twice, a back game strategy.

THE ROLL: 6–2   (Diagram 18)
Again you can start moving one of your back men and again you can be hit twice by Red, although this time his chances of hitting are increased as not only will 5–4 × enable him to hit but also 4–4. This move can lead to either a running game strategy or a back game strategy, depending on whether or not you are hit twice.

4. BUILDING-RUNNING MOVES (B-RM)

THE ROLL: 6–4   (Diagram 19)
This move may lead either to a combination of a blocking-running strategy (if Black is not hit) or to a back game strategy if he is hit.

THE ROLL: 6–3   (Diagram 20)
Again Black may move into either a blocking-running strategy or, if he is hit, a back game strategy.

THE ROLL: 6–2   (Diagram 21)
The principle is the same – if Black is not hit he may move into a blocking-running game strategy or, if the worst happens, into a back game strategy.

THE ROLL: 5–4   (Diagram 22)
This move, provided Black escapes being hit, may lead him to a running strategy or gives him the possibility of making Red's most important point – the 5-point.

THE ROLL: 5–1   (Diagram 23)
Again provided Black is not hit he may move into a running strategy or have the possibility of making Red's 5-point.

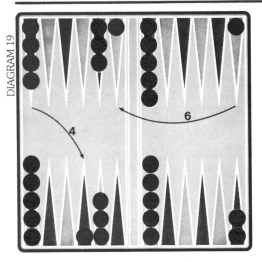

DIAGRAM 19

THE ROLL: 6–4

THE MOVE: 24 → 18, 13 — 9
TYPE OF MOVE: B–R.M.

No of blots left: 3
No of ways to hit those blots: 36
No of ways of not hitting those blots: 0
Odds in your favour: —
Odds against you: —
% in your favour: —
% against you: 100% being hit once

Recommended

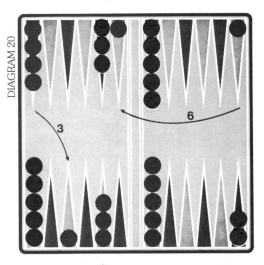

DIAGRAM 20

THE ROLL: 6–3

THE MOVE: 24 → 18, 13 → 10
TYPE OF MOVE: B–R.M.

No of blots left: 3
No of ways to hit those blots: 36
No of ways of not hitting those blots: 0
Odds in your favour: —
Odds against you: —
% in your favour: —
% against you: 100% being hit once

Recommended

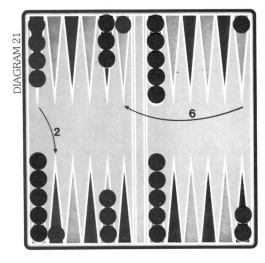

DIAGRAM 21

THE ROLL: 6–2

THE MOVE: 24 → 18, 13 → 11
TYPE OF MOVE: B–R.M.

No of blots left: 3
No of ways to hit those blots: 36
No of ways of not hitting those blots: 0
Odds in your favour: —
Odds against you: —
% in your favour: —
% against you: 100% being hit once

Recommended

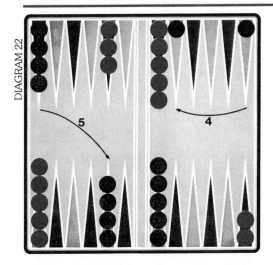

THE ROLL: 5–4

THE MOVE: 24 → 20, 13 → 8
TYPE OF MOVE: B–R.M.

No of blots left: 2
No of ways to hit those blots: 32
No of ways of not hitting those blots: 4. (6–4) × ;
  (4–2) ×
Odds in your favour: —
Odds against you: 8 to 1 being hit once
% in your favour: —
% against you: —

Recommended

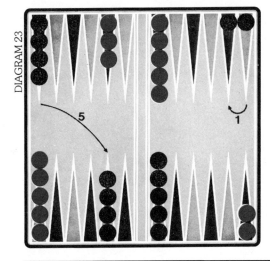

THE ROLL: 5–1

THE MOVE: 13 → 8, 24 → 23
TYPE OF MOVE: B–R.M.

No of blots left: 2
No of ways to hit those blots: 34
No of ways of not hitting those blots: 2. (2–1) ×
Odds in your favour: —
Odds against you: 17 to 1 being hit once
% in your favour: —
% against you: —

Recommended (for beginners as well)

THE ROLL: 4–3 (Diagram 24)
As in the previous two moves if Black is not hit he may be led into a running strategy, but he still has the possibility of making Red's 5-point.

THE ROLL: 4–3 (Diagram 25)
Here Black has merely reversed his previous move – in fact it has the same effect. If he is not hit, it may lead to a running strategy; again he is in a position to make Red's 5-point.

THE ROLL: 4–1 (Diagram 26)
Black splits his back men and brings a builder round 4 points. This may, once again, lead him into a running strategy if his blot remains unharmed and Red's 5-point can still be made.

THE ROLL: 3–2 (Diagram 27)
If not hit, Black may go into a running strategy or he can make Red's 5-point.

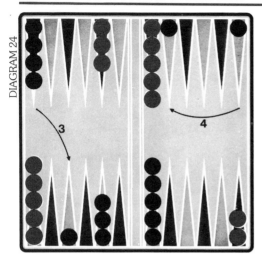

THE ROLL: 4–3

THE MOVE: 24 → 20, 13 → 10
TYPE OF MOVE: B–R.M.

No of blots left: 3
No of ways to hit those blots: 32
No of ways of not hitting those blots: 4. (6–4) × ;
  (4–2) ×
Odds in your favour: —
Odds against you: 8 to 1 being hit once
% in your favour: —
% against you: —

Recommended

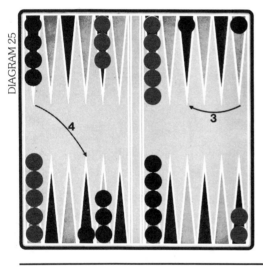

THE ROLL: 4–3

THE MOVE: 13 → 9, 24 → 21
TYPE OF MOVE: B–R.M.

No of blots left: 3
No of ways to hit those blots: 36
No of ways of not hitting those blots: 0
Odds in your favour: —
Odds against you: —
% in your favour: —
% against you: 100% being hit once

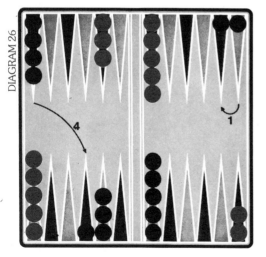

THE ROLL: 4–1

THE MOVE: 13 → 9, 24 → 23
TYPE OF MOVE: B–R.M.

No of blots left: 3
No of ways to hit those blots: 34
No of ways of not hitting those blots: 2. (2–1) ×
Odds in your favour: —
Odds against you: 17 to 1 being hit once
% in your favour: —
% against you: —

Recommended (for beginners as well)

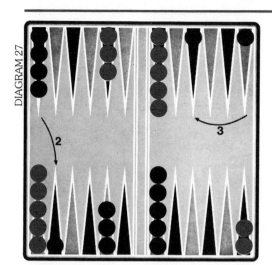

DIAGRAM 27

THE ROLL: 3–2

THE MOVE: 24 → 21, 13 → 11
TYPE OF MOVE: B–R.M.

No of blots left: 3
No of ways to hit those blots: 36
No of ways of not hitting those blots: 0
Odds in your favour: —
Odds against you: —
% in your favour: —
% against you: 100% being hit once

Recommended

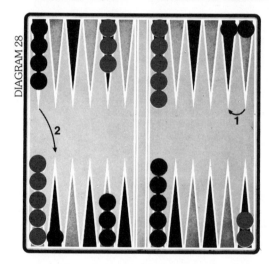

DIAGRAM 28

THE ROLL: 2–1

THE MOVE: 13 → 11, 24 → 23
TYPE OF MOVE: B–R.M.

No of blots left: 3
No of ways to hit those blots: 34
No of ways of not hitting those blots: 2. (2–1) ×
Odds in your favour: —
Odds against you: 17 to 1 being hit once
% in your favour: —
% against you: —

Recommended (for beginners as well)

THE ROLL: 2–1   (Diagram 28)
This move may lead Black into a running strategy, if his blot is not hit, or give him the chance of making the 5-point in Red's homeboard.

5. CHANCE MOVES (CM)
THE ROLL: 6–2   (Diagram 29)
Here you are mainly concerned with trying to develop a blocking game strategy by making your 5-point (provided of course that you are not hit). It's true that Red has 15/36 chances of hitting the blot but he may not use 1–1 or 3–1 × preferring to make his bar- and 5-points, or the 5-point, with those rolls. Thus the chances of his hitting you are reduced to 12/36.

6. BUILDING-CHANCE MOVES (B-CM)
THE ROLL: 5–1   (Diagram 30)
A similar principle applies here. If Black escapes being hit then he can use one of his extra builders to make his 4-point. This move may then lead to a blocking game strategy.

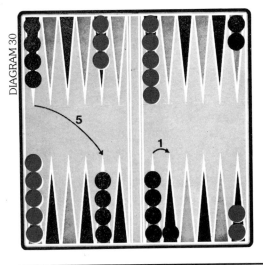

THE ROLL: 6–2

THE MOVE: 13 → 5
TYPE OF MOVE: C.M.

No of blots left: 1
No of ways to hit those blots: 15. (6–4) × ; (5–4) × ;
    (4–3) × ; (4–2) × ; (4–1) × ; (3–1) × ; (1–1); (2–2);
    (4–4)
No of ways of not hitting those blots: 21
Odds in your favour: 7 to 5 against being hit
Odds against you: —
% in your favour: —
% against you: —

Recommended

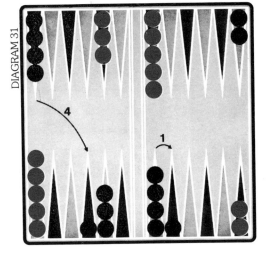

THE ROLL: 5–1

THE MOVE: 13 → 8, 6 → 5
TYPE OF MOVE: B–C.M.

No of blots left: 1
No of ways to hit those blots: 15. (6–4) × ; (5–4) × ;
    (4–3) × ; (4–2) × ; (4–1) × ; (3–1) × ; (1–1); (2–2);
    (4–4)
No of ways of not hitting those blots: 21
Odds in your favour: 7 to 5 against being hit
Odds against you: —
% in your favour: —
% against you: —

Recommended

THE ROLL: 4–1

THE MOVE: 13 → 9, 6 → 5
TYPE OF MOVE: B–C.M.

No of blots left: 2
No of ways to hit those blots: 19. (6–4) × ; (6–2) × ;
    (5–4) × ; (5–3) × ; (4–3) × ; (4–2) × ; (4–1) × ;
    (3–1) × ; (1–1); (2–2); (4–4)
No of ways of not hitting those blots: 17
Odds in your favour: —
Odds against you: ᴗ 1 to 1 being hit once
% in your favour: —
% against you: —

Recommended

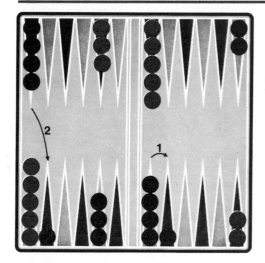

THE ROLL: 2–1

THE MOVE: 13 → 11, 6 → 5
TYPE OF MOVE: B–C.M.

No of blots left: 2
No of ways to hit those blots: 15. (6–4) × ; (5–4) × ;
    (4–3) × ; (4–2) × ; (4–1) × ; (3–1) × ; (1–1); (2–2);
    (4–4)
No of ways of not hitting those blots: 21
Odds in your favour: 7 to 5 against being hit once
Odds against you: —
% in your favour: —
% against you: —

Recommended

THE ROLL: 4–1   (Diagram 31)
If neither of Black's blots are hit then this move may develop into a very strong blocking game strategy. (Work out for yourself what throws you need to make your 5- or bar-points, or both!)

THE ROLL: 2–1   (Diagram 32)
Once again Black is trying to develop a strong blocking game strategy and provided he does not get his blots taken off the board he has a good possibility of succeeding.

III

The Response

Planning the response to the opening move is the second step in the strategy of the game (the first step being the opening move itself). Mathematically speaking there are 315 responses to all the opening moves (15 opening moves × 21 responses to each opening move). Don't forget that a double roll cannot be used for an opening move and is therefore only counted among the responses.

Let's have a look first at the double rolls and the best way to play them. For the moment we shall ignore the opening move and just look at the double roll in question.

THE ROLL: 1–1   (Diagram 33)
Move two men from your 8-point to your bar-point and another two men from the 6-point to the 5-point. You have now produced half a prime.

THE ROLL: 2–2   (Diagram 34)
Move two men from your 6-point to your 4-point, and two men from the 24-point to the 22-point. With this move you are combining blocking and running. Alternatively instead of moving your back men you could move two men from your 13-point to your 11-point. This move would then be a pure blocking move.

THE ROLL: 3–3   (Diagram 35)
Move two men from the 8-point to the 5-point and move with your back men from the 24-point to the 21-point, combining blocking and running. Instead of moving the back men you could make an extra point in your homeboard by moving two men off the 6-point to the 3-point. This move is a pure blocking move.

THE ROLL: 4–4   (Diagram 36)
Move two men from the 13-point to the 9-point and move the back men from your 24-point to your 20-point – once again this is a combination of blocking and running.

THE ROLL: 5–5   (Diagram 37)
Unless your opponent has split his back men this is a very poor move for you. All you can do is to move two men all the way from point 13 to point 3.

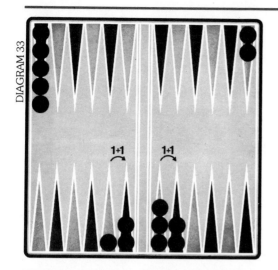

DIAGRAM 33

THE ROLL: 1–1

THE MOVE: 8 → 7 (2 men), 6 → 5 (2 men)
TYPE OF MOVE: P.M.

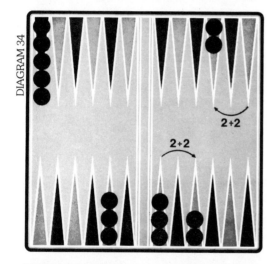

DIAGRAM 34

THE ROLL: 2–2

THE MOVE: 24 → 22 (2 men), 6 → 4 (2 men)
TYPE OF MOVE: P.M.

DIAGRAM 35

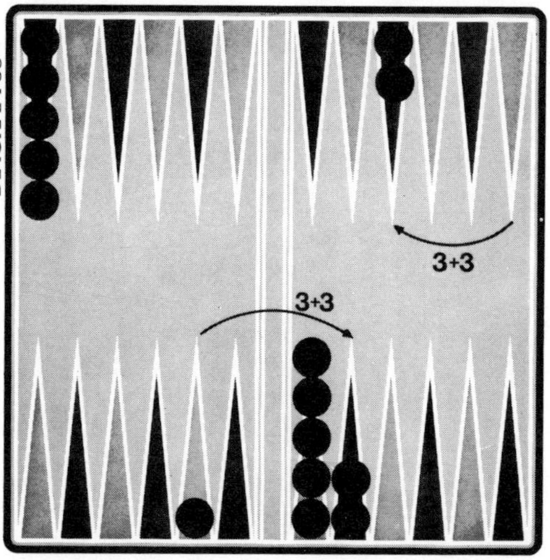

THE ROLL: 3–3

THE MOVE: 24 → 21 (2 men), 8 → 5 (2 men)
TYPE OF MOVE: P.M.

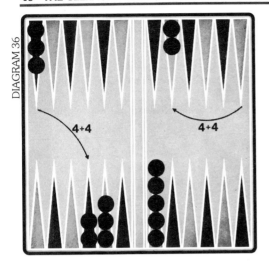

THE ROLL: 4–4

THE MOVE: 13 → 3 (2 men)
TYPE OF MOVE: P.M.

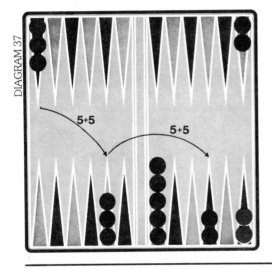

THE ROLL: 5–5

THE MOVE: 24 → 20 (2 men), 13 → 9 (2 men)
TYPE OF MOVE: P.M.

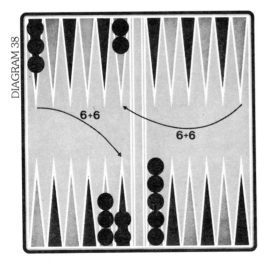

THE ROLL: 6–6

THE MOVE: 24 → 18 (2 men), 13 → 7 (2 men)
TYPE OF MOVE: P.M.

THE ROLL: 6–6   (Diagram 38)

Move two men from your 13-point to make your bar-point, and move the back men from point 24 to make your opponent's bar-point (your 18-point).

In practice however we can't always play the ideal move; your opponent's opening move will obviously affect your response. You must always try to anticipate what your opponent is going to do and you must certainly understand why you are planning to move the way you are. Now, let's work out the responses to the opening moves that were recommended for beginners. (NB: if no particular play is shown for a double roll then play it as shown at the beginning of this chapter.) First of all, the recommended opening moves for beginners were:

Roll	Diagram		Roll	Diagram		Roll	Diagram
3–1	6		5–2	12		6–3	17
6–1	7		4–3	13		6–2	18
4–2	8		3–2	14		5–1	23
5–3	9		6–5	15		4–1	26
5–4	10		6–4	16		2–1	28

THE RESPONSE TO OPENING MOVE 6–1

Assume your opponent has played the opening roll 6–1 as shown in Diagram 7. Now, you roll:

6–5 Move two men from your 13-point, one to your bar-point and one to the 8-point.

4–3 Play the four with one of your back men and move one man from your 13-point to your 10-point.

3–2 Play the three with one of your back men and move one man from your 13-point to your 11-point.

2–2 Move your back men all the way to your 20-point.

6–6 Make your bar-point and your 2-point.

Any roll other than these may be played as recommended for beginners.

THE RESPONSE TO OPENING MOVE 3–1   (Diagram 6)

You have rolled:

4–4 Make your 5-point with two men from your 13-point.

All other rolls should be played as recommended for beginners.

THE RESPONSE TO OPENING MOVE 4–2   (Diagram 8)

With:

2–2 Make your opponent's 5-point.

3–3 Make two points in your homeboard, point 5 and point 3.

Play all other rolls as recommended for beginners.

THE RESPONSE TO OPENING MOVE 5–3   (Diagram 9)

With:

2–2 Make your 4-point and your 11-point.

Every other roll should be played as recommended for beginners.

THE RESPONSE TO OPENING MOVE 6–5   (Diagram 15)

If your opponent has played this opening move as recommended then with:

2–2 Make your opponent's 5-point.

3–3 Make your opponent's bar-point.

5–5 Make your 3-point and your 1-point, hitting on the 1-point at the same time.

5–4 Play the four with one of your back men then move one man from your 13-point to your 8-point.

4–3 Use one of your back men to play the four and one man from point 13 to play the three.

3–2 One of your back men plays the three and one man from your 13-point plays the two.

All other rolls should be played as recommended for beginners.

THE RESPONSE TO OPENING MOVE 6–4   (Diagram 16)

Assuming your opponent has played this move as recommended then with:

6–4 Make your 2-point.

6–3 Move one of your back men to your opponent's bar-point and one man to your 10-point.

6–2 Hit on your 11-point and move one of your back men to your opponent's bar-point.

5–4 One of your back men goes to your opponent's 5-point and one man goes from your 13-point to your 8-point.

5–2 Hit twice – on your 11-point and on your 1-point.

4–3 Use a back man to play the four and a man from point 13 to play the three.

4–2 or **3–2** Hit on your 11-point, and play the four or the three with one of your back men.

2–2 Make your 11-point, and hit and make your 4-point.

5–5 Make points 3 and 1, hitting on 1 at the same time.

All other rolls should be played as recommended for beginners.

THE RESPONSE TO OPENING MOVE 6–3   (Diagram 17)

If your opponent has played the opening move as shown then with:

6–4 Make your 2-point.

6–3 Hit the blot on your 10-point.

6–2 Bring one man from your 13-point to your 5-point.

5–4 As before, one of your back men moves the four and one man from point 13 plays the five.

5–3 Hit twice – on points 10 and 1.

5–2 Use one of your back men to play the two and one man from your point 13 to play the five.

4–3 Hit on your 10-point and play the four with one of your back men.

3–2 Hit on your 10-point and play the two with one of your back men.

2–1 Hit on your 10-point.

2–2 Make your opponent's 5-point.

3–3 Make your 10-point, hitting at the same time, and make your 5-point.

5–5 Make two points, 3 and 1, hitting on the 1 at the same time.

All other rolls to be played as recommended for beginners.

THE RESPONSE TO OPENING MOVE 6–2   (Diagram 18)

If your opponent has played this as shown in the diagram then with:

6–4 Hit on your 9-point with the four and move one of your back men to your opponent's bar-point with the six.

6–3 Run with both back men.

5–4 Hit twice.

5–2 One back man plays the two and one from point 13 the five.

4–3 or **4–2** Hit on your 9-point and move one of your back men.

3–2 or **2–1** Run with both back men.

2–2 Hit on your 9-point and make your 4-point.

4–4 Make your 5-point, hitting the blot on your 9-point on the way.

   All other rolls should be played as recommended for beginners.

THE RESPONSE TO OPENING MOVE 5–4   (Diagram 10)

If your opponent has moved as shown then with:

2–2 Make your opponent's 5-point.

4–4 Hit the blot on your 15-point and make your 4-point.

   All other rolls may be played as recommended for beginners.

THE RESPONSE TO OPENING MOVE 5–2   (Diagram 12)

Your opponent has played as shown and you roll:

6–2 Bring one man all the way to your 5-point.

2–2 Make your opponent's 5-point.

   The remaining rolls should be played as recommended for beginners.

THE RESPONSE TO OPENING MOVE 4–3   (Diagram 13)

If your opponent played this roll as recommended with:

5–3 Hit the blot on your 15-point.

2–2 Make your opponent's 5-point.

4–4 Hit the blot on your 16-point and make your 4-point.

   All other rolls to be played as recommended for beginners.

THE RESPONSE TO OPENING MOVE 3–2   (Diagram 14)

If your opponent has played this as recommended with:

6–2 Bring one man all the way to your 5-point.

2–2 Make your opponent's 5-point.

   All other rolls to be played as recommended for beginners.

THE RESPONSE TO OPENING MOVE 5–1   (Diagram 23)

If your opponent has played as recommended then with:

6–4 Make your 2-point and hit.

5–4 or **4–3** Play a build-run move, using one of your back men to play the four.

3–2 Play the three with one of your back men and the two to your 11-point.

3–3 Make your 3-point and your 10-point.

4–4 Make your 2-point, hitting at the same time, and make your 4-point.

5–5 Make two points, 3 and 1, hitting on the 1 at the same time.

   All other rolls to be played as recommended for beginners.

THE RESPONSE TO OPENING MOVE 4–1   (Diagram 26)

If your opponent has played as recommended then with:

6–4 Make your 2-point, hitting at the same time.

5–3 Hit on your point 16.

4–1 Hit twice in your homeboard.

3–3 Make your 3-point and 10-point.

4–4 Hit the blot on your point 16 and make your point 2, hitting again.

5–5 Make two points in your homeboard, 3 and 1, hitting on the 1.

   All other rolls should be played as recommended for beginners.

THE RESPONSE TO OPENING MOVE 2–1 (Diagram 28)

Your opponent has played as shown and you roll:

2–2 Make your opponent's 5-point.

4–1 Hit twice in your homeboard.

4–4 Hit on point 16, and make point 2, hitting again.

3–2 Play the three with one of your back men and the two to your point 11.

3–3 Make your 3-point and your 10-point.

5–5 Make two points in your homeboard, 3 and 1, hitting on the 1 at the same time.

All other rolls should be played as recommended for beginners.

To help you work out the best response to the other opening moves in Chapter II, I have drawn up a table as shown below in Table 7. At the top of each column write the relevant opening move. In the left hand column I have listed all the possible rolls, so all you have to do is ask yourself the 'chain of questions' and then write down the response you think best in each case. If you want to jot down your reasons the column on the right is blank. The more you practice the better and you should soon find yourself automatically able to work out the best response to any opening move.

TABLE 7: THE RESPONSE

THE ROLL	1	2	3	4	5	REMARKS
6–5						
6–4						
6–3						
6–2						
6–1						
5–4						
5–3						
5–2						
5–1						
4–3						
4–2						
4–1						
3–2						
3–1						
2–1						
1–1						
2–2						
3–3						
4–4						
5–5						
6–6						

IV

Bearing Off Strategy

First, some basic information. In the situation shown in Diagram 39 Black has to play 2–2. See what you would do with this move (and why) and then check it with the correct move.

If you use three of the 2s to bear off one man from the 6-point (how you use the fourth is really irrelevant) then the only way you can end the game on your next roll (assuming you have another roll) is by throwing either double 6 or double 5. However if you move the two men on point 6 to point 4 and the two men on point 5 to point 3, then – if you do have the chance of another roll – you also have an extra chance of finishing the game, i.e. with double 4. Only by moving all four men down two points each would you be able to take advantage of this extra winning roll.

Now Black has to play 5–1. How would you move? Work it out first and then check the answer.

Obviously the 5 must be used to bear one man off the 5-point. But what about the 1? You should move the man on the 3-point to the 2-point. This will give you the extra winning shot of 2–2; any other move is therefore incorrect. So you will see that it is not always right to move from the highest point down.

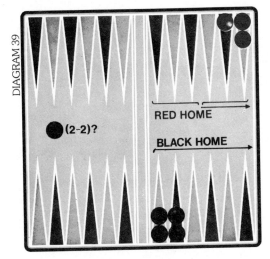

DIAGRAM 39

(2-2)?

RED HOME

BLACK HOME

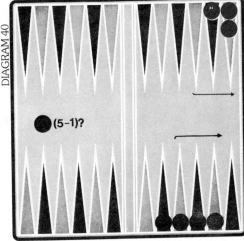

DIAGRAM 40

(5-1)?

In Diagram 41 it is now Red to play and he has rolled 1–1. How would you move? Again work it out before checking with the correct answer below.

You must take the man off your 1-point – this is essential in order to leave you with only four men – and then move all three men from the 4-point down to the 3-point. This will give you the extra roll of 3–3 which you wouldn't otherwise have, had you borne off two men (always assuming of course that you get the chance of another roll).

Conclusion: As you can see it is not always correct play to bear off as many men as you can. If all you need is a double to end the game, then sometimes leaving yourself with four men instead of three will give you a better chance.

In Diagram 42 Black has to play 6–2. Again work it out for yourself before looking at the answer. (If you want some help have another look at the section in Chapter I dealing with the probability of bearing off the last two men in one roll.)

In Diagram 43 Red has to play 6–2. There is no doubt that the 6 must be used to save the blot in Black's outerboard, but where should the 2 be played? Does it really make any difference? Well, we can check. Red has two options: one, he can move the blot all the way to his bar-point as shown in Diagram 44. Now, what's the worst that can happen to Red on his next roll? Well, should he roll 6–6 he will be forced to leave a blot exposed either to a 5 (on his 8-point) which will give Black 13/36 chances to hit (any 5: 11/36, plus (4–1) × : 2/36) or to a 4 on his bar-point giving Black only 11/36 chances. But Red can also play this roll another way as shown in Diagram 45. By playing in this way Red now has everything under complete control. He *cannot* leave a blot on his next roll whatever he may throw!

Conclusion: If you don't have to give a shot – even at a 35 to 1 chance – then don't. If Red had played as shown in Diagram 44 and Black managed to hit and cover the blot in his home-board, then Red would be in real trouble. In the actual game from which this example is taken, Red played as shown in Diagram 45.

In Diagram 46 Black has a 3–1 to play and has at least two options. One, as shown in Diagram 47; if Black plays by moving his blot all the way, then on his next roll, should he roll a 6–4 ×, he is going to be forced to leave a blot either on his 5-point or two blots – one on the 9-point and one on the 2-point (3/36 chances). Check it for yourself. Two, Black can play this move as shown in Diagram 48. Playing this way, only 6–5 × will force him to leave a blot on his 5-point (2/36 chances – one less than before).

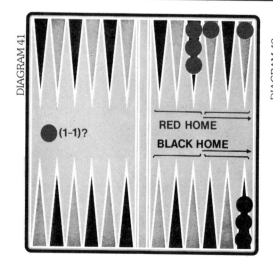

DIAGRAM 41

(1-1)?

RED HOME

BLACK HOME

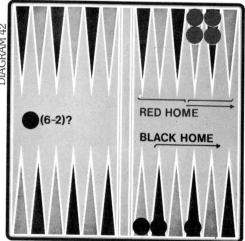

DIAGRAM 42

(6-2)?

RED HOME

BLACK HOME

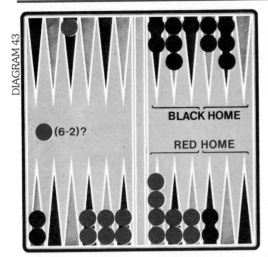

DIAGRAM 43

BLACK HOME

RED HOME

(6-2)?

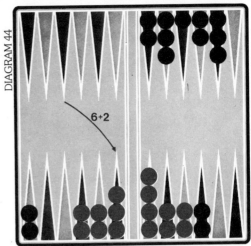

DIAGRAM 44

6+2

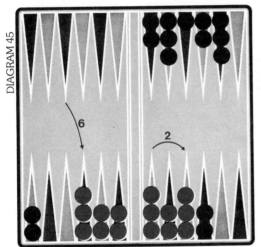

DIAGRAM 45

6

2

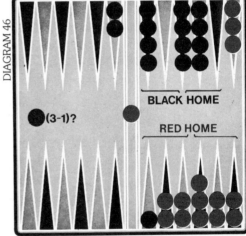

DIAGRAM 46

BLACK HOME

RED HOME

(3-1)?

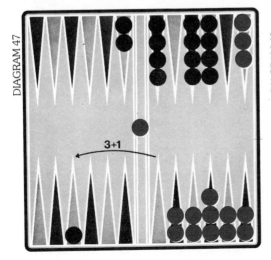

DIAGRAM 47

3+1

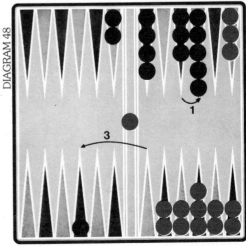

DIAGRAM 48

1

3

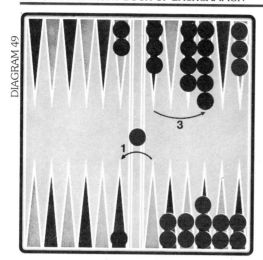

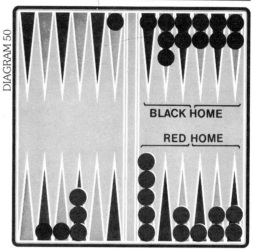

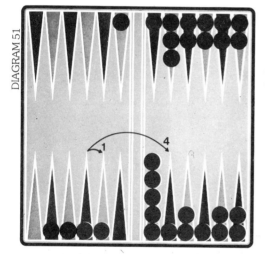

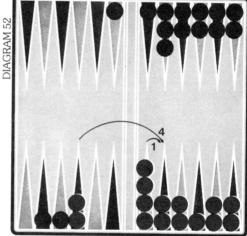

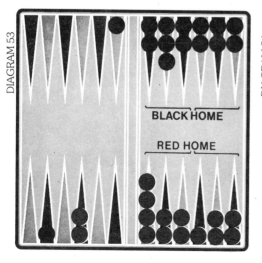

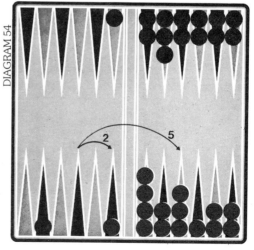

You may now be asking yourself 'why not move the blot 1 pip and play the 3 with a man from point 6?' That would put you in the position shown in Diagram 49.

There are at least three good reasons why you should not make such a move.

1. The most important one: by playing the 3 in this way Black is losing a vital builder off his 6-point and should he now roll 1–1 he would not be able to utilize this very good roll to make two important points in his homeboard (5 and 2), assuming of course that Red has not already been able to make the 5-point with a roll of 5–4 (don't forget that Red has a man on the bar waiting to come in).

2. When your opponent is holding your 1-point you must try and pile most of your men on the highest points in your homeboard, *not* the lowest, so that you are able to play most rolls without having to leave a blot too early.

3. It will be much more problematical for Black to bring in a blot safely so far behind.

In the actual game, the move was played as shown in Diagram 48. Black was thus taking a 'controlled risk' rather than an unnecessary one.

Conclusion: Always try to avoid taking an unnecessary risk (Diagram 45) and if you do have to, make it a 'controlled' one, as in Diagram 48.

In Diagram 50 Red now has to play 4–1. One possible play is to move with two men from his outerboard – one in with the 4 and one up with the 1, as shown in Diagram 51.

The other is to bring one man in with the 4, and then to move one man down from the 6-point to the 5-point as shown in Diagram 52.

This is the correct play because Red is slightly ahead (74 pips as opposed to Black's 77, and it is Red to move) so he must take this opportunity to distribute his men more evenly in his homeboard. Remember, in this type of bearing off it is extremely important to have at least two men on each point so that you can bear off the maximum of two with a regular roll every time, whilst trying to avoid leaving the lowest points vacant during the process of bearing off. In the actual game Red played as shown in Diagram 52, taking advantage of the fact that he is nearer to his homeboard than Black is to his.

Now in Diagram 53 it's Red's turn again and he has to play 5–2. (His pips now total 66 to Black's 68 and it's his move.) One play is to bring in one man with the 5, and to move the other man to his bar-point with the 2, as shown in Diagram 54.

But you can see immediately that Red is going to have to roll constantly high numbers if he is to keep the lead. He is very weak on his 6-point with so many men there. An alternative play is shown in Diagram 55.

Here, as before, Red has used the 5 to bring one man in but with the 2 he has moved from the 6-point to the 4-point. Having done this the only roll that can be bad for him is 2–1, which would only enable him to bring the last man in. However, as he is ahead – Black still has two men to bring in, one of them needing a long shot – and the chances against rolling 2–1 are 17 to 1 it is worth his while to take the risk. This is therefore the correct play. On the other hand, should Red have been behind, then the correct play would have been as shown in Diagram 55. In the actual game the move was played as shown in Diagram 54. Well, even an 'expert' sometimes makes a mistake!

In Diagram 56 Black has thrown 3–1. In the actual game he took one man off the 3-point and moved one man from the 6-point to the 5-point, as shown in Diagram 57.

The correct move, though, would have been to bear one man off the 4-point, thus avoiding leaving two low points vacant, and leaving the board looking like Diagram 58.

In Diagram 59 Black has to play 6–4.

In the actual game the move was played as shown in Diagram 60.

This means that Black, should he in his next roll throw either 5–5 or 2–2, will only be able to take off two men. If he had played as shown in Diagram 61, then 5–5 or 2–2 will take off three

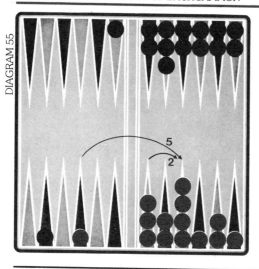

DIAGRAM 55

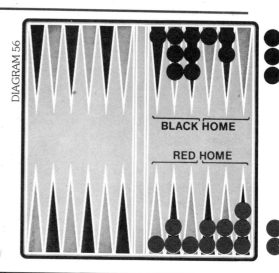

DIAGRAM 56

BLACK HOME

RED HOME

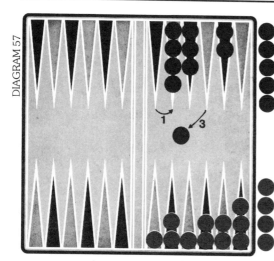

DIAGRAM 57

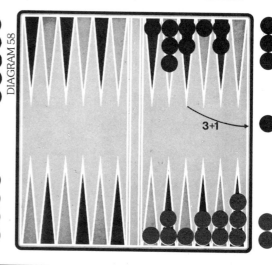

DIAGRAM 58

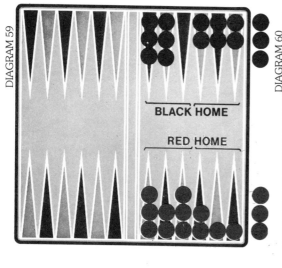

DIAGRAM 59

BLACK HOME

RED HOME

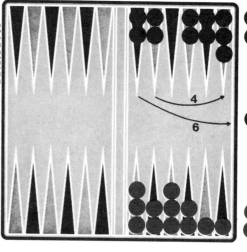

DIAGRAM 60

men. The remaining rolls would have the same result in both cases but why deprive yourself of the extra chance unnecessarily?

Conclusion: Always bear in mind that when you are behind you should try and bear off as many men as you can, and when you have to move within your homeboard (i.e. when you cannot bear off two men with a regular roll or four with a double) then move from the highest point down. However if you are ahead, then think about your next roll, move to give yourself the maximum number of chances and avoid leaving the lowest points vacant.

In Diagram 62 Black has to play 2–1. It was played by bearing one man off the 3-point as seen in Diagram 63.

The correct move would have been to bear off one man from point 2, and move one man from point 6 to point 5. Playing thus enables three men to be borne off with 5–5 or 3–3 as opposed to only two, while at the same time you are moving down on to the lowest points, leaving the board in the position in Diagram 64.

Conclusion: You must always anticipate your next roll, giving yourself the maximum opportunity to use it fully. But it is even more important here to take advantage of your lead to

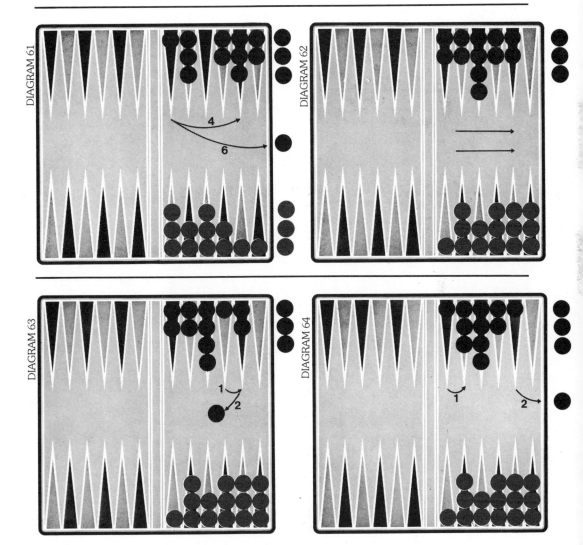

strengthen your position, moving down from the highest points without weakening the lowest ones.

In Diagram 65 Black has to play 5–1.

In the actual game the move was played by bearing off with the 5 and moving one man to point 3, leaving as bad rolls 6–5, 6–2, and 5–2 (6/32 chances). This was quite correct. Had Black moved with the 1 to point 4, then the bad rolls would be 6–4, 6–3, 5–4, 5–3, 4–2, 3–2, or 4–4 (13/36 chances). Work it out for yourself by studying the board in Diagram 66.

In Diagram 67 Black has a 4–3 to play. If he plays both numbers from the 5-point as shown in Diagram 68, then on the next roll he will be forced to leave a blot with 6–1, 5–1, 4–1, or 3–1, (8/36 chances), and will have to leave two blots with 6–3 or 5–3 (4/36 chances), giving a total of 12/36 chances for Red to have a shot.

However if Black plays as shown in Diagram 69, then he has to leave a blot if he next rolls 6–2, 5–2, 4–2, 3–2, or 3–1 (10/36 chances) or two blots if he rolls 6–3 (2/36 chances) again giving a total of 12/36 chances for Red to hit. But the play in Diagram 69 decreases Black's chances of leaving two blots on his next roll – and that you should always try to avoid. In the actual game the roll was played as shown in Diagram 68.

In Diagram 70 Red has to play 2–1. If he plays as shown in Diagram 71, and this was how the move was played in the actual game, then 5–4 will force him to leave a blot (2/36 chances) and with 6–5 he will be forced to leave two blots (another 2/36 chances) giving a total of 4/36 chances of his leaving at least one blot on his next roll. However if he had played as shown in Diagram 72, then on his next roll only 6–5 or 4–4 could have forced him to leave a blot – and then only one – and the chances (3/36) are less than in the previous play. In addition, Red still only needs seven rolls to finish (although he took one man off before, it did not affect the number of rolls needed to end the game) provided of course that all goes well. So, you are not always bound to increase your chances of winning by bearing off an extra man. Always remember that if you leave two blots and your opponent manages to hit one of them, you are bringing him back into the game. If he then hits your second blot as well then it is highly probable that you will lose the game – and why risk that when you are so near to victory?

In Diagram 73 Red has to play the unpleasant roll of 6–2.

He can do this in two ways. First, as shown in Diagram 74.

If Red plays like this then Black has only to throw any 3 (11/36 chances) to hit Red's blot, and very probably he will then go on to win the game. Should Black fail to hit on this roll, and

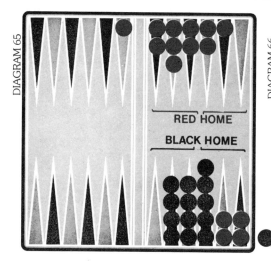

RED HOME

BLACK HOME

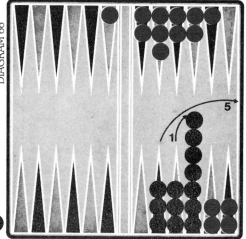

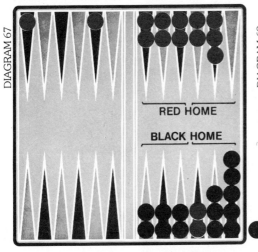

RED HOME

BLACK HOME

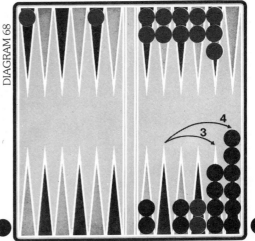

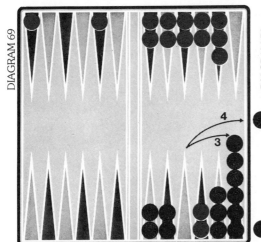

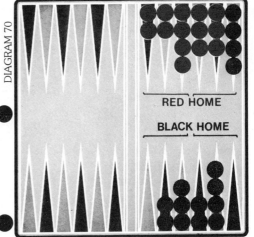

RED HOME

BLACK HOME

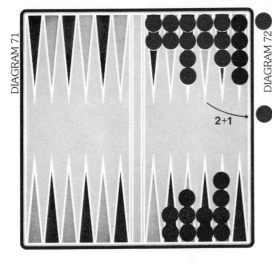

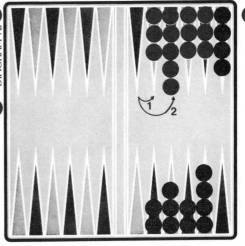

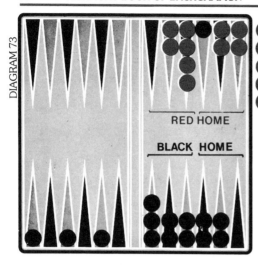

DIAGRAM 73

RED HOME

BLACK HOME

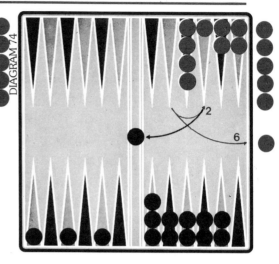

DIAGRAM 74

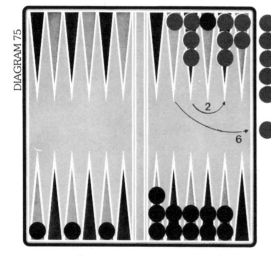

DIAGRAM 75

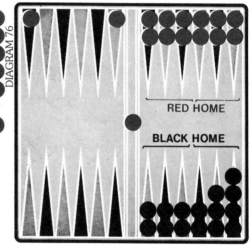

DIAGRAM 76

RED HOME

BLACK HOME

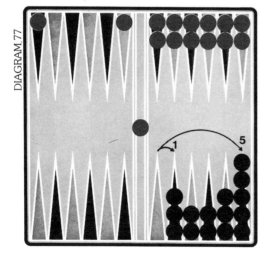

DIAGRAM 77

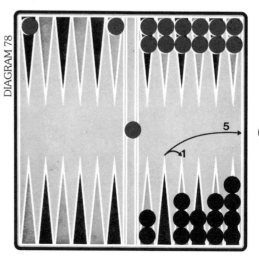

DIAGRAM 78

Red on his next roll throws 6–5, 6–4, 5–4, 3–3, 4–4, 5–5, or 6–6, then he is still forced to leave a blot (11/36 chances). But if Red plays as shown in Diagram 75, Black can still win the game should he roll any 2 (11/36 chances: 1–1 will not help him). Should he fail to hit Red, then Red is safe, because there is no roll that will force him to leave a blot. Obviously this second play is the better of the two; it was the way in which the move was played in the actual game.

In Diagram 76 Black has to play 5–1. No doubt you may often have asked yourself when in this situation (or when your opponent is holding your 1-point) how can one best distribute the men in order to avoid leaving a blot? Before giving a concrete answer – if indeed there is one – let's see how this roll can be played (Diagram 77).

Black may move both men off his 6-point, and if Red now gets in, Black's problems are over. However if Red fails to throw a 6, then Black will have to leave a blot on his next roll should he throw 6–5, 6–4, 5–4, 5–3, 4–3, 4–4, 5–5, or 6–6 (11/36 chances). On the other hand if Black plays as shown in Diagram 78, and Red fails to enter with 5 (11/36 chances) then Black only has to leave a blot with 6–1, 5–1, 4–4, 5–5, or 6–6 (7/36 chances – four less than before). If Red does manage to come in and decides to stay there (a good decision) then only 6–1 and 5–1 will force Black to leave a blot that Red can hit (4/36 chances); if Red doesn't now throw the requisite 1 (11/36 chances) then Black on his next roll can go behind Red and lose contact – something he is anxious to do as quickly as possible.

So what is the answer to our question about the best possible distribution of men? Well, the first thing to do is check your opponent's homeboard. If it is closed as shown in Diagram 76 then Black should play as shown in Diagram 77 because even though he may leave a blot, what he is trying to do is lose contact quickly. If on the other hand Red's board is not closed, then Black should play as in Diagram 78, because now Black wants to keep his chances of being hit to a minimum. If he does have to leave a blot and Red fails to hit it, then he can go behind Red and his problems are over.

Conclusions: If your board is closed and your opponent has a man on the bar, try to have an even number of men on your highest points (with three men on your 6-point and two on your 5-point a roll of 6–5 will force you to leave a blot), so either have two men on your 6-point and two on your 5-point, or three men on each point. This of course is different from when your opponent is holding your 1-point. Then we saw that it was vital to pile your men on the highest points (6, 5, 4) so that you could play most rolls without having to leave a blot, while at the same time hemming your opponent in and possibly giving yourself a double game.

Always try to work out your moves so that you do not have to leave a blot until you have, say, at least ten men off the board. If you can delay it even further, until your last man, then your chances of winning are approximately 18 to 1 in your favour. In this case you will either offer a double which your opponent will most probably refuse; or if the doubling cube is on his side, and you cannot force him out of the game in this way, then you are favourite anyway to win a single game.

One last word – take your time. Never rush during the bearing off process while you still have contact with your opponent.

V

The Structure of the Game

PARTS OF THE GAME (See TABLE 8)

PART I OPENING OF THE GAME

This is the beginning of the game and consists of first, the opening move; second, the response to the opening move; and third, the next one or two moves, by which time the player has come into a position which will decide his choice of the type of game he should play. This decision is vital. That is why it is so important to play the opening move and response correctly, remembering all we looked at in the previous chapters.

PART II MIDDLE OF THE GAME

Once you have made up your mind what type of game to play, stick to it (unless an unusual development occurs), or you will find yourself with no strategy at all. In this part of the game you must remember what we said earlier about leaving blots, where to put builders, and so on. It is during this stage that developments may force you to change strategies, or more likely, to mix them. This we shall see later.

PART III END OF THE GAME

Part III, not unnaturally, follows straight on from Part II. The end of the game will develop according to the type of strategy you have adopted. Therefore the end of a running game will obviously look different from the end of a blocking game, or from the end of a back game. Included in this part is the last roll dealt with previously under 'bearing off'.

One must remember that in some games it will be easy to identify the three different parts and in others very difficult. But the mere fact that you are looking at the game and trying to distinguish the different stages will at least put you on the right road to becoming a good player.

We shall look first at the pure strategies (having briefly identified the mixed strategies), then see how to move into a mixed strategy and to what extent strategy is influenced by the doubling cube. We shall do this from the point of view of the player who is making the decisions and adopting one kind of play as opposed to another, and then we shall deal with the defence against these strategies.

At this stage, if you want to know what to do against a certain strategy, then remember that in general what is good for Player A is not good for Player B, and vice versa.

To be able to decide when and how to change strategy or how to mix two different ones, we must be familiar with the pure strategy of each type of game, but first let's just quickly identify what the mixed strategies are.

Mixed Strategy

The pure strategy of each type of game will not, in fact, carry us very far when playing the actual game. Therefore we shall have to learn how to mix pure strategies in order to produce a 'grand strategy'. Mathematically, there are three different types of grand strategy, although in practice there are only two. At this stage we are dominating the game and our decision will therefore be an offensive one. (We shall look at defence in the next chapter.)

1   Combination of Running and Blocking Games

This combination includes everything that you will find in the pure strategies of running and blocking games. Basically, while trying to block your opponent's back men you must also advance your own back men. It is important therefore to keep your leading roll. So avoid being hit, otherwise you may lose the lead you have. This combination can give the best results, and possibly even a gammon.

2   Combination of Blocking and Back Games

Here you have not managed to run with both your back men, but you have managed to produce half a prime and are trying to block at least one of your opponent's back men. Keeping contact in this case is important; you must try not to lose it until you have freed your blocked man or men, and that won't be until your opponent has broken his home board.

3   Combination of Running and Back Games

These two types of game contradict each other, so in fact cannot be combined into a grand strategy. But once you have managed to bring your back men out safely there is no reason to play a back game.

Let's look now at the development of each of the pure strategies.

TABLE 8: THE STRUCTURE OF THE GAME

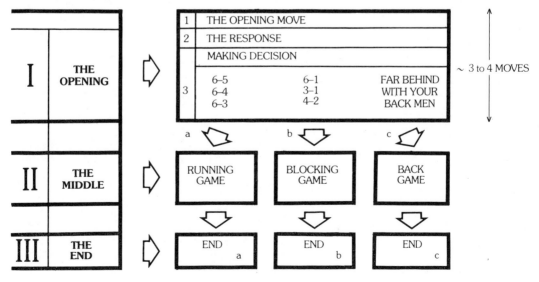

Pure Strategy
SECTION A. THE RUNNING GAME

We saw at the beginning of the chapter how to decide when to adopt a running strategy. Remember, it is always a good idea to do so if you can. That's one of the secrets of good backgammon – try to run with your back men as quickly as possible. The faster you can run, the more the game will turn in your favour. But you must bear certain factors in mind:

1. If you are one roll ahead, try to keep it that way throughout the game.

2. Try to have your men more advanced than those of your opponent.

3. Reduce your chances of being hit as much as possible so that you don't lose your advantage.

4. Avoid hitting blots. Remember you are aiming to lose contact as quickly as you can, so you don't want your opponent's men behind you. More especially you don't want his men in your homeboard, because it will make it more difficult for you to enter your men safely. It is crucial that you know how to move towards losing contact, and above all to know exactly when actually to lose it. The moment you decide to do so you must try and enter your homeboard as quickly as possible, in order to start bearing off first. But meantime you must not forget the importance of distributing your men properly. If you start piling most of them on points 6 and 5, hoping for miracle rolls of double 6 and double 5 all the time, you'll discover all too soon that miracles don't happen! (See Chapter IV.) Now let's have a look at a typical running game, and see the strategy in practice.

In Diagram 79 Red has opened with 6–5 and has moved one back man all the way to his point 13.

Black in turn has rolled 4–4. He moves his back men to make Red's 5-point, and two others to make his own 9-point, thus trying to slow down Red's advance (Diagram 80).

In Diagram 81 Red rolls 6–3. He must run with his remaining back man in order not to find himself suddenly trapped in Black's homeboard.

Black then rolls 5–2 – a crucial moment for him, and he must think very carefully before moving. Red has one blot in Black's outerboard, so if Black decides to hold on to Red's 5-point, Red may then save this blot and move very definitely into the lead. So Black must now run with one of his back men to safety (to his point 13, as in Diagram 82).

If Red should now roll 3–1, 1–1, or 4–4 (4/36 chances) he will most probably hit, and make a point, on Black's blot. However with any other roll he will almost certainly try to save his own blot thus keeping his lead. So Black's decision to run is quite right – he is taking 8 to 1 chances against being hit. Diagram 82 shows a typical situation where both players are involved in a running game; from now on they will each try to save their respective blots and enter their homeboards as quickly as they can.

In another actual game a very interesting position arose. Both players were in a partial running game waiting for the right moment to lose contact, when Red rolled 6–5 – a 'difficult' roll in the situation shown in Diagram 83.

Red cannot take a chance and move the 6 from his 10-point, because that would leave a blot exposed to any 5 (15/36 chances for Black to hit); and with Black's good board, if Red is hit now he will quite probably lose the game. So he has two alternatives, one as shown in Diagram 84, which will give Black the opportunity to hit with 6–3, 5–4, 5–3, 4–3, 3–2, 3–1, 2–1, 1–1, and 3–3 (16/36 chances); or he can play as shown in Diagram 85 – which is obviously much better.

Now Black can hit with only 6–4, 6–3, 5–4, or 3–3 (7/36 chances, 9 less than before). But what is much more important to notice is that Black can only hit with a long shot, which would force him to leave a blot in Red's homeboard. Red, on the other hand, if not hit on the next roll, may now swing the game in his favour.

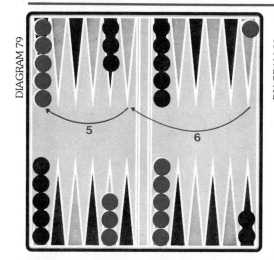

DIAGRAM 79

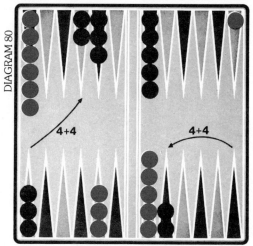

DIAGRAM 80

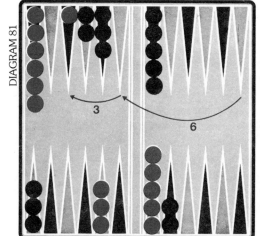

DIAGRAM 81

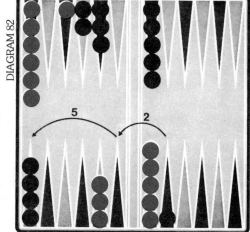

DIAGRAM 82

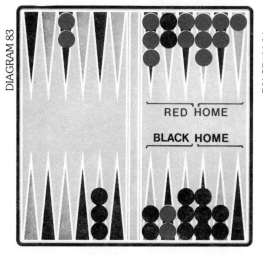

DIAGRAM 83

RED HOME

BLACK HOME

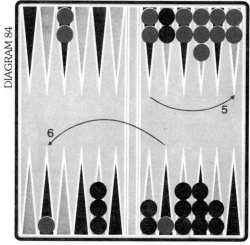

DIAGRAM 84

In the actual game, the move was played as shown in Diagram 85; and then a few moves later Black found himself facing the same problem. The position had reached the stage in Diagram 86 when Black rolled 6–3. The pip count before this roll was:

Red – 84, Black – 86, and it's his roll.

He can play the move in three different ways. One, he can play safe as shown in Diagram 87.

However, this will mean that any 6 Black rolls now (excluding doubles) will force him to leave a blot either in Red's homeboard (with 6–5 or 6–1 he would have to leave his man on Red's 5-point) or in Red's outerboard (should he roll 6–4, 6–3, or 6–2). Therefore it's not advisable to move like this. The second possibility is for Black to run all the way with one of his back men, as in Diagram 88; Red can hit Black if he rolls 6–5, 6–1, 5–4, 5–3, 5–2, 5–1, 4–1, 3–2, 3–1, 2–1, 1–1, or 5–5 (22/36 chances, even though he might choose not to hit with some of those rolls as they would then force him to leave either one or two blots in his homeboard). The other choice Black has is to move both men off Red's 5-point (Diagram 89). Thus Black is not only decreasing his chances of being hit (Red can now hit only with any 2 or double 1 – 12/36 chances and 10 fewer than before) but he is also increasing his chances of losing contact, provided of course that the blot is not hit, when he could then take advantage of his faster board.

So I repeat – if you possibly can, try to develop a running strategy right from the beginning of the game.

SECTION B. THE BLOCKING GAME

The object of this type of strategy is to block your opponent's back men as quickly as possible (or man, should he have managed to escape with one man very near the beginning of the game). To do so you must build a blockade in anticipation of your final aim – a prime. Once you have managed to produce half a prime you must next bring builders into your outerboard in order to enlarge the blockade; and once you have built your prime and managed to block your opponent's man or men, then you must try not to break it. As you need twelve men to produce a prime you must have at least one of your remaining three men able to play a long shot so that the prime can be kept intact. Sometimes you will find that the best place for you to be, in order to maintain your prime, is on the bar! Even if your opponent manages to close his board he cannot start bearing off since you have at least one of his men trapped. To clarify these points let's have a look at some examples from actual games.

In Diagram 90 Black has to play 6–5, which is disastrous. It doesn't matter what he does – he is going to have to leave two blots. Analyse this example carefully and see if you can work out a way for Black to prevent such a situation. (He should have kept at least one man in Red's outerboard.)

In another actual game, as shown in Diagram 91, Red had to play 3–1.

Well, there is no choice about the 1 – Red must come in off the bar. But what about the 3? If Red plays safe by moving one man from his bar-point to his 4-point then he not only gives Black a chance to cover the blot on his 5-point, but, should he fail to roll a 6 next time enabling him to escape with his back man, then he will be forced to break his prime. It is therefore a much better idea to play this roll as shown in Diagram 92.

As before, Red has entered with the 1, but he uses the 3 to hit on his 2-point. Either way, whether or not Red is hit, this play is to his advantage: he has more chance of maintaining his prime and he may even collect another of Black's men!

In another game, shown in Diagram 93, Red is trying to block his opponent's back men and has to play 4–3.

Black holds three points in his homeboard while Red has only two in his, but Red has managed to make his bar-point. That's why, in the actual game, he played as shown in Diagram 94.

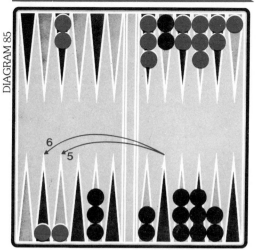

DIAGRAM 85

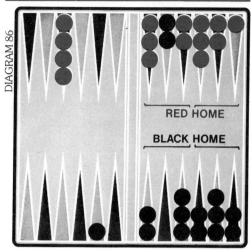

DIAGRAM 86

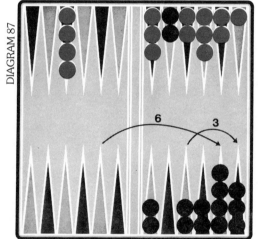

DIAGRAM 87

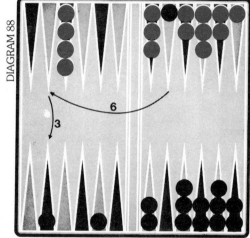

DIAGRAM 88

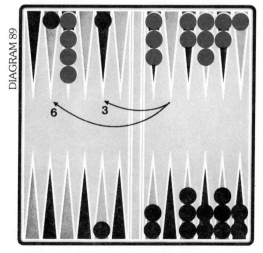

DIAGRAM 89

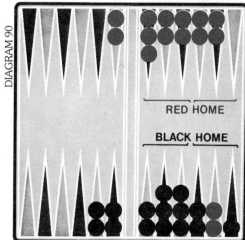

DIAGRAM 90

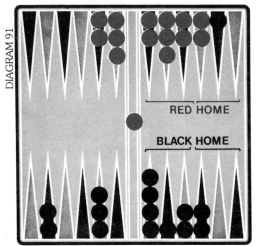

DIAGRAM 91

RED HOME

BLACK HOME

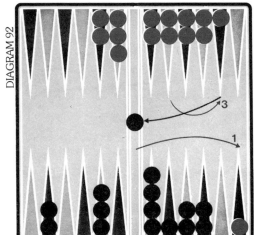

DIAGRAM 92

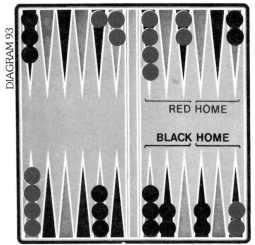

DIAGRAM 93

RED HOME

BLACK HOME

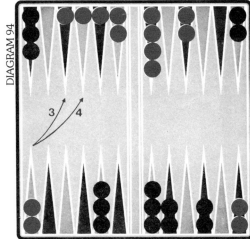

DIAGRAM 94

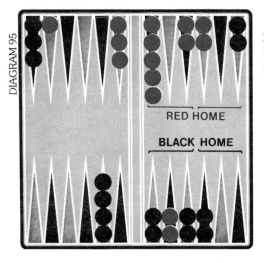

DIAGRAM 95

RED HOME

BLACK HOME

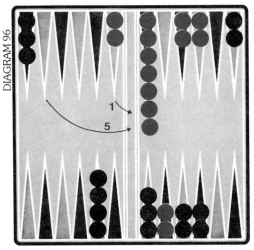

DIAGRAM 96

This is very aggressive play by Red – Black has 11/36 chances of hitting (with 6–2, 6–1, 5–4, 5–2, 4–3, and 4–4) – but if he is not hit then he is in a very good position to develop a proper blocking game. In Diagram 95 we have a typical example where a risk *must* be taken in order to try to produce a blockade. Red has to play 5–1; he can play safely by moving his blot to his 6-point (with the 5) and moving a man from his bar-point to his 6-point (with the 1) as shown in Diagram 96.

You can see immediately how poor this play is. True, Red is safe, but what has he achieved? Absolutely nothing. On his next roll, should he throw a 6 (excluding double 6) Red will have to break Black's 5-point and leave at least one blot that Black could hit, and quite likely two. So there is only one way for Red to play to swing the game in his favour, and that's by taking a chance as shown in Diagram 97.

It is true that Black now has 13/36 chances of hitting (any 4 plus 3–1) but even then Red is secure because he is holding a point in Black's homeboard. If he is not hit, then on his next roll he has 21/36 chances of covering the blot on his 5-point and thus producing a 5-point blockade. (Red's 21 chances are: 6–2, 6–1, 5–2, 5–1, 4–2, 4–1, 3–2, 3–1, 2–1, 1–1, 2–2, and 5–5.) Here Red is taking a 'controlled' risk in order to improve his position ultimately. Why 'controlled'? Well, should he be hit he has a point in his opponent's homeboard to come back to: try to remember this kind of combination. (You are taking a 'controlled' risk when you have an anchor in your opponent's homeboard.)

Lastly, let's look at another actual game where a player chose to play a blocking game strategy. Black has started with the opening move 5–2 as in Diagram 98.

Red then rolled 2–2. It would not be a bad idea for Red to make his 4-point and at the same time move his two back men up (Black has an extra builder in his outerboard which may enable him to make his bar-point, thus blocking Red's back men). But instead Red played the roll as shown in Diagram 99.

By doing this Red is signalling to his opponent that he is going to try to develop a blocking strategy. Black then rolled 3–1 and made his 5-point, shown in Diagram 100, while Red next rolled 3–3. The fact that Black has managed to make his 5-point is now forcing Red to think about his back men; but instead of running with both of them to Black's bar-point, Red decided to give up his blocking strategy and to combine blocking and running at the same time. (Diagram 101). Playing in this way, Red still has opportunities to enlarge his blockade, and for the moment he need not worry too much about his back men.

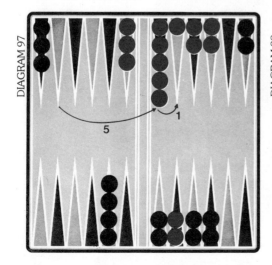

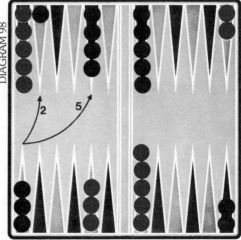

DIAGRAM 99

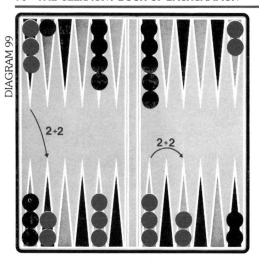

DIAGRAM 100

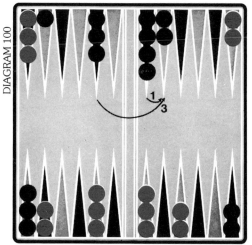

DIAGRAM 101

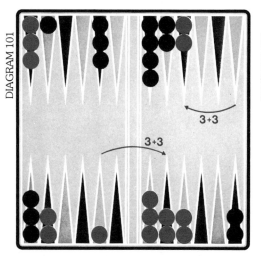

DIAGRAM 102

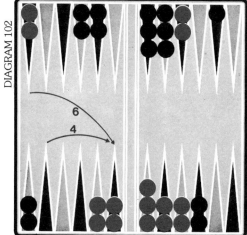

DIAGRAM 103

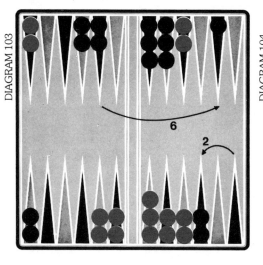

DIAGRAM 104

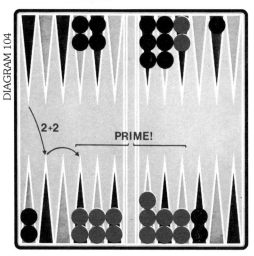

Black then rolled 4–2 and made his 9-point, while Red rolled 2–1 and made his 8-point (leaving a blot on his 11-point). Black's next roll was 2–1 which he played by moving one of his back men 2 and one man from his 6-point to his 5-point. Red then rolled 6–4 and made his bar-point so that the board now looked like Diagram 102.

Black rolled 6–2, and played as shown in Diagram 103.

Playing the 2 by moving up the back man was a must. Next Red rolled 2–2 and managed to produce a prime – Diagram 104.

Study this game again from the beginning, and learn how to come to a position (in other words to swing the game in your favour) as quickly as possible.

SECTION C. THE BACK GAME

You may remember that we said at the beginning of this chapter that you must sometimes – primarily when you are too far behind to be able to win in the ordinary way – adopt a back game strategy. Before looking at the actual strategy, let's see how a player may become involved in such a game. In one that took place at the Clermont Club during the first World Backgammon Cup Duplicate Tournament in October 1973, one of the players opened with 4–1 played as in Diagram 105.

A question arises here – why did Red play the 1 so as to leave a blot exposed to a direct shot? Well, he is hoping to be able to develop a blocking strategy by coming to a position as quickly as possible.

Let's go on with the game. Black then rolled 6–4, a good roll enabling him to run with one of his back men and hit at the same time (Diagram 106).

Next, Red rolled 6–3. He must enter on the 3, but the 6 is a problem, which brings us to the question of the back game strategy. We shall look at this first, and then come back and see how Red should play in this particular instance.

The strategy of the back game is really the reverse of the running game. In the latter your aim is to lose contact as quickly as possible in order to start bearing off first. In the back game it is essential to keep contact until the last moment, which is why it is so important that you hold your opponent's 1-point (or at least have a blot there). Why? Well, your opponent has fifteen men to bear off: suppose that he has managed to take off fourteen of them in seven rolls (we are excluding here the possibility of double rolls) and is now left with one man as illustrated in Diagram 107.

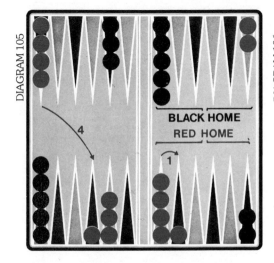

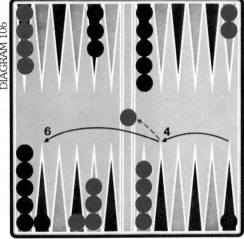

DIAGRAM 107

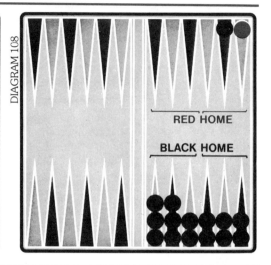

RED HOME

BLACK HOME

DIAGRAM 108

RED HOME

BLACK HOME

DIAGRAM 109

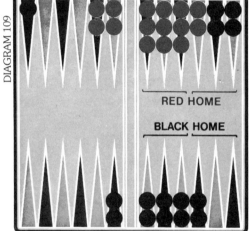

RED HOME

BLACK HOME

DIAGRAM 110

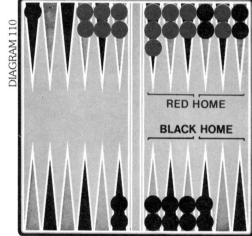

RED HOME

BLACK HOME

DIAGRAM 111

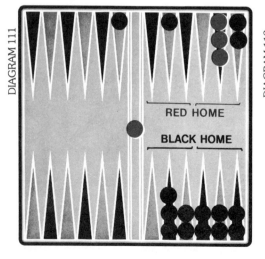

RED HOME

BLACK HOME

DIAGRAM 112

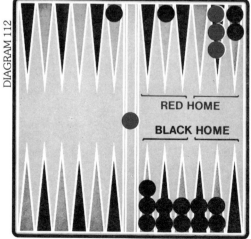

RED HOME

BLACK HOME

Black has only to throw a 1 (any 1 will do) to hit Red's blot and save a gammon. His chances of doing so are 11/36 or approximately 2 to 1 against. If he rolls the unfortunate combination of 3–2 however, then he will be backgammoned. If though the situation had been as it is in Diagram 108, then only a double 6 could save Black from a gammon. These two situations demonstrate the two main facts about a back game: firstly, do not go into a back game deliberately, because the odds are that you will lose a double game. Secondly, once circumstances have forced you into a back game, then go right back and secure your opponent's 1-point – it is absolutely vital if you are to have any chance at all! However, vital though this point is, it is not quite enough on its own. To have a proper back game you must hold at least one other good point in your opponent's homeboard; the best points to have are the 1- and 3-points or the 1- and 2-points. Let's have a look at Diagram 109.

Here Red will leave a blot if he rolls 6–5 or 6–4, while a roll of 6–6 will not enable him to move at all. So he has four shots that may cost him the game. In Diagram 110, Black is holding the 1- and 3-points. Here if Red should roll 6–5 he will have to leave two blots, while with 6–6 he can only play half the move (with the two men on the 8-point). In both cases, if Red is hit it may cost him the game but only in one situation: if Black has his board properly built from the highest points down. Why? Well, let's have a look at Diagram 111.

Here, Black has managed to hit and put Red on the bar. Red now needs any 6 to enter (11/36 chances) and, having entered, any roll (36/36 chances) will take him out of Black's homeboard. Although Black may be able to hit again it will probably be very difficult now for him to win the game. But if Black's homeboard looks like the one in Diagram 112, then Red still has 11/36 chances to enter with any 1, but once in he now needs a 6 to get him out of Black's board which is 25 chances fewer than he had previously. Black is therefore obviously in a much better position to win.

These last two examples are good illustrations of the 'timing' of a back game. It's true that in Diagram 111 Black had the opportunity of another shot at Red while involved in a back game but that was only part one. Part two – to hit – is more difficult! Even if Black should be able to hit again, without being prepared for it, i.e. without having built up his homeboard as in Diagram 112, it may not help to win the game. In other words good timing means prepare yourself for the moment you have an opportunity to hit.

Let's return now to Diagram 106. Red rolled 6–3 and was forced to enter with the 3. But what should he do with the 6? He now has three men at the back. If he tries to come out with the man recently entered off the bar he will merely be giving Black more opportunity to hit at the same time, bettering Black's position. So the correct play for the 6 is illustrated in Diagram 113.

Red has played to his bar-point for two reasons. In a back game (and the sooner you can identify what type of game you are playing the better, as you can then adopt the appropriate strategy and play accordingly) you must slow yourself down: that is you must first try to establish two good points in your opponent's homeboard and then start building your own board. Red has encompassed both these objectives with his play. If he is hit then he has a chance of making Black's 3-point, thereby producing the perfect back game position; and if he is not hit then he may make his own bar-point and have a partial prime, thus combining the blocking and back game strategies. Black's next roll was 6–1 and he quite correctly made his bar-point as in Diagram 114. (See Chapter VI, Section C).

Next Red rolled 6–1. Obviously he must make his bar-point but should he use the 6 or the 1? He is faced here with either making a proper blockade, or with forcing Black to hit him and slow him down (which is exactly what he wants) so he plays as shown in Diagram 115.

Should Black on his next roll throw any 4, he must hit Red's blot on the 5-point, thus helping Red slow himself down and giving him the possibility of making Black's 3-point. If Black doesn't hit then Red may make his 5- or 9-point (or both) and Black will be in real trouble! So as far as slowing yourself down is concerned in the back game, always try to use men from the 6-point

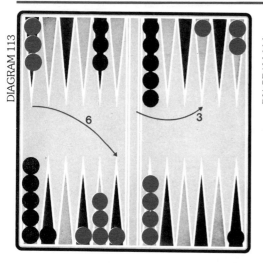

DIAGRAM 113

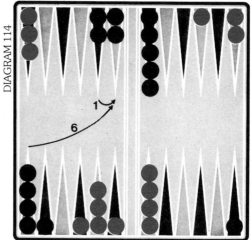

DIAGRAM 114

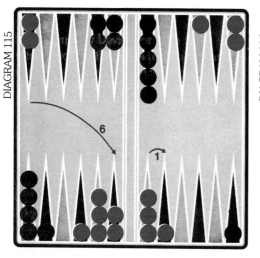

DIAGRAM 115

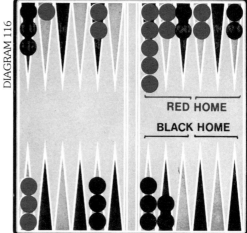

DIAGRAM 116

RED HOME

BLACK HOME

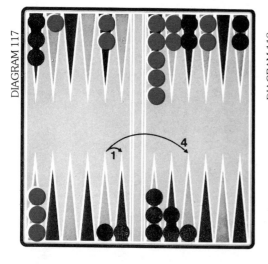

DIAGRAM 117

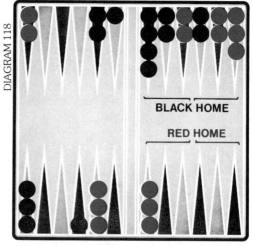

DIAGRAM 118

BLACK HOME

RED HOME

because they need three rolls to bring them home again (remember – the average roll is eight points). Thus you can always work out how fast or slow you are and adjust your play accordingly.

So, to recap: once you realise you are going to be involved in a back game, leave as many blots as possible, forcing your opponent to hit you so you can establish two good points in his homeboard. Then start building your own homeboard from the highest points down – at this stage you must be slow and your opponent fast, so to keep yourself slow have as many men as you can in your opponent's outerboard. Then long shots will not destroy your back game by forcing you to come out too early. Double 6 or 5 are particularly to be guarded against – they can be absolutely disastrous rolls.

Let's have a look now at Diagram 116.

Black has to play 4–1. An analysis of his position shows that he has established two points in Red's homeboard (not as good as the points we mentioned before but nevertheless two points) so now he must concentrate on building his own homeboard; the priority here is obviously point 4. So the correct play is as illustrated in Diagram 117.

Black is building up his board in the correct way while keeping as many men back as he can in Red's outerboard in case he has long shots.

When you find yourself too fast and you know you must try to slow down, how do you do it? One way is to hit, if you can. In the situation shown in Diagram 118 Red has rolled 6–3. How should he play? He has a very good position for a back game, holding three points in Red's homeboard, but precisely because of this he is in fact already too fast – and yet he is not ready to hit Black as he has no board. But the only way to achieve the three objectives important to him *is* by hitting Black. This may appear contradictory but just look at it. If Red hits Black on Black's bar-point and then drops one man on his own 5-point, as shown in Diagram 119, he stops Black making his own bar-point (and that is a vital one for Black); he slows himself down (a must if he is to keep his good back game position); and thirdly, if not hit on the 5-point he may make it on his next roll, thus starting to build his board.

Another way of slowing down by forcing your opponent to hit you is demonstrated in the example in Diagram 120.

Here Red has to play 4–3. If you remember we said that in a blocking game your aim is to produce a prime of closed points, at the same time blocking one (at least) of your opponent's men. The strategy here though is slightly different – what you are aiming for now is a 'prime of blots', with your opponent behind you so that he must hit and so help you slow your game down.

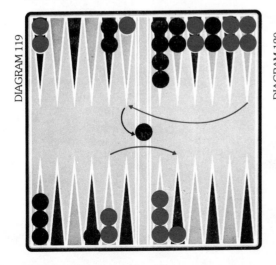

DIAGRAM 119

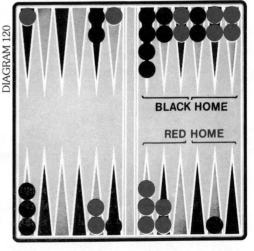

DIAGRAM 120

BLACK HOME

RED HOME

He is not particularly keen on doing so, but like it or not he has to get out and will probably have to hit you in the process. Therefore the correct play in this situation is as Diagram 121. Study this position carefully – it will help you to develop your own ideas on how to build a back game.

Sometimes your timing may be perfect: i.e. you have established yourself in your opponent's homeboard and your own homeboard is well built, yet your opponent is far from starting to bear off – what do you do then? Let's look at the situation in Diagram 122: Black has to play 6–2. Before seeing how he should play let's just check Red's position. He has a blot on his 2-point and four more men to bring in. His main aim therefore is to cover the blot and avoid leaving any more. If we assume for a moment that it is Red to play then 6–5, 6–3, 6–2, 4–3, 4–1, 3–2, 3–1, 1–1, 3–3, 4–4, and 6–6 (18/36 chances) will enable him achieve his aim, so in other words it is even money that Red will not leave a blot on his next roll. Black has two different aims: he doesn't want to lose his opportunities of hitting and he doesn't want his game to become too fast. In the actual game the move was played as shown in Diagram 123.

Was this correct? Well, Red's chances of not leaving a blot are marginally improved (he has double 2 available to him now) but Black still has his back game position and he has a better defence now against large doubles (two men as opposed to one in Red's outerboard) so it *was* the right play.

You should start to move out of your back game position only when it is going to improve your situation. Let's look at another example that demonstrates when you should do so. (Diagram 124). Here Red has to play 4–1. If you study the diagram carefully you will see that there is only one correct way for Red to play, as shown in Diagram 125.

There are three reasons for this. First, Red is still maintaining his good homeboard. Secondly, he is decreasing the chance of losing a double game (should he not have the opportunity to hit Black). Thirdly, and most important, he is putting Black in a very awkward position should he now roll 6–3, 5–3, 3–2, 3–1, 4–3, or 4–2 (12/36 chances). With these rolls Black can either bear off one or two men or hit Red's blot – in both cases leaving a blot of his own, while if he should be so unlucky as to roll 6–4 or 5–4 then he has to leave two blots. So there are 16 in 36 chances that Black will leave at least one blot.

It is important as we said before to identify quickly what type of game you are involved in so that you can develop the right strategy properly. The paradox of the back game is that one should avoid playing it if possible, yet the best time to start is at the beginning when your opponent has, as yet, no board. However, if you have the opportunity of delaying going into a back game, then do delay. The next example, Diagram 126, illustrates this point.

Red rolled 3–1. He must enter off the bar and he must also hit Black on his 5-point to prevent Black making this vital position. He can do this in two ways, first as shown in Diagram 127.

Playing thus Red is definitely committing himself to a back game. He is well blocked with four men at the back (and will quite likely have a fifth any minute now). But if he plays as Diagram 128, he is delaying going into a back game (he still has plenty of time and a good position should he eventually need to do so) and the man brought in with the 3 can now, if necessary, come out with a direct 6 and possibly even hit. He has also made maximum use of his builders on the 6-point.

And lastly, another example of when to come out of the back game position – Diagram 129. Here Black has to play 2–1. Well, he couldn't have hoped for a better roll – not only can he hit, but he can make his 5-point too.

In Diagram 130 Black still has a point in his opponent's homeboard and is in a very good position to switch from a back game strategy to a blocking one. But, once again, check carefully the two positions before you decide to come out of a good back game situation.

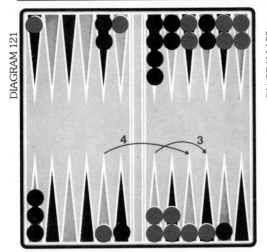

DIAGRAM 121

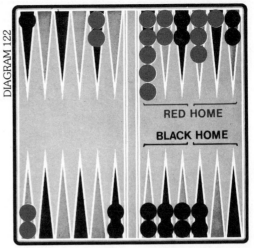

DIAGRAM 122

RED HOME

BLACK HOME

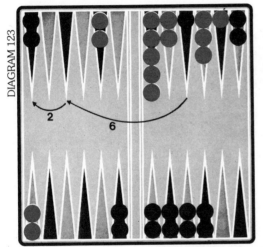

DIAGRAM 123

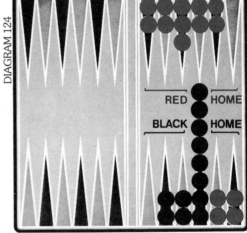

DIAGRAM 124

RED HOME

BLACK HOME

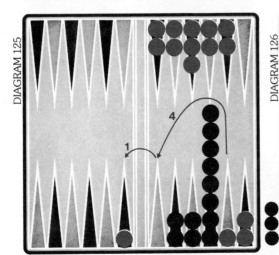

DIAGRAM 125

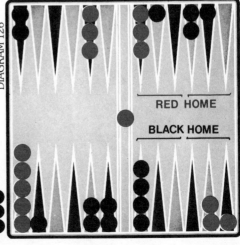

DIAGRAM 126

RED HOME

BLACK HOME

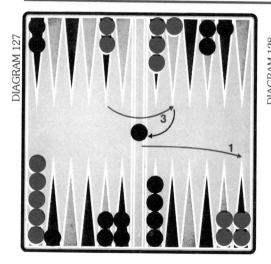

DIAGRAM 127

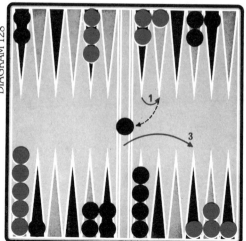

DIAGRAM 128

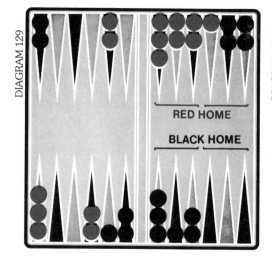

DIAGRAM 129

RED HOME

BLACK HOME

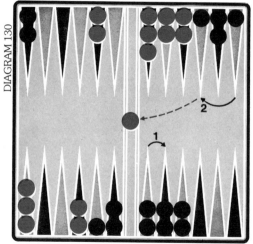

DIAGRAM 130

VI

Defence

SECTION A. HOW TO PLAY AGAINST A RUNNING GAME

The first thing you have to do is to check that you are not too far behind (use one of the counting systems to do so). If your opponent's lead is not great (say not more than 20 pips and it's your roll), then you must try to adopt a running strategy and thus cancel your opponent's lead. If you are well behind, then try first to play a partial blocking game; that is, try to keep contact, because that's what your opponent wants least. At the same time build as many points as you can in your outerboard to slow his advance. If possible force him to leave a blot so that you can hit and nullify his advantage. If none of these options is open to you, then (but *only* then) move into the 'hitting process', and develop a proper back game strategy. Remember that once your opponent has embarked on a running game, he is unlikely to want to change strategy – so you must try to force him to do so.

Let's look at some examples to clarify these points. In Diagram 131, Red has to play 2–2. He can play as shown in Diagram 132; with this move he is trying to slow Black's advance (by blocking 6–6 for Black's back men) while also moving forward himself with his own back men so as not to find them blocked. But because Black is holding Red's 5-point it would be much better in this instance for Red to play as shown in Diagram 133.

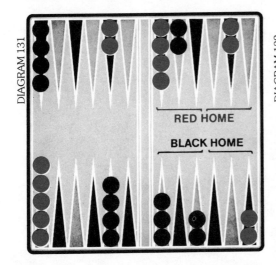

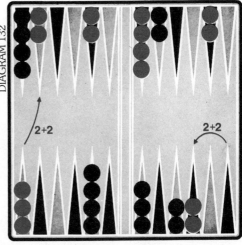

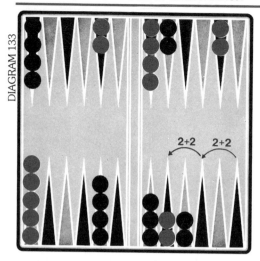

DIAGRAM 133

DIAGRAM 134

BLACK HOME

RED HOME

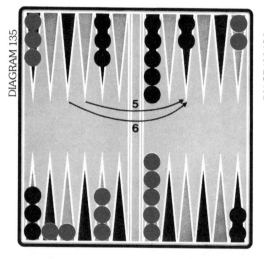

DIAGRAM 135

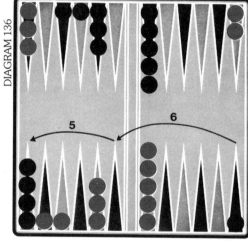

DIAGRAM 136

DIAGRAM 137

RED HOME

BLACK HOME

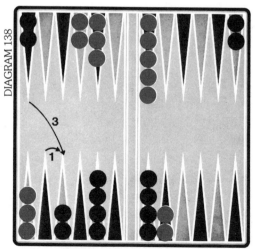

DIAGRAM 138

Now Red holds Black's 5-point, thus cancelling Black's former advantage. So you can see that the running game is preferable here to partial blocking strategy. In the actual game the move was played in this way.

In Diagram 134 Black has to play 6–5. If he plays as shown in Diagram 135 he is making maximum use of his blots to establish his 4-point, and is trying to develop a blocking strategy; but he is totally ignoring the situation on the other side of the board! Red has enough builders to make either his bar- or 5-point, or both, so Black may find himself blocked with two men at the back. Therefore the correct play is for Black to prevent this by running with one of his back men to safety (Diagram 136).

The blots that Black has left in his outerboard are only exposed to long shots, standing less chance of being hit (check the 'inconvenient probability'); if they are not hit (and his back man escapes Red's attentions) then he may be able to use them to block Red's back men, provided of course that Red doesn't escape in the meantime.

In Diagram 137 Black has to play 3–1. Black is behind and he also has a blot that Red can hit with any 6 (excluding 3–3) – so Black must try to slow Red down and at the same time save his blot if he can. The only way to do both things is for Black to make his 10-point (Diagram 138) and that's exactly what Black did in the actual game.

SECTION B. HOW TO PLAY AGAINST A BLOCKING GAME

When your opponent has started to block your back men (say he has managed to make his bar- or 5-point) the first thing you must try to do is run with one of your back men or at least to split them. Why? Well, your opponent will almost certainly attempt to enlarge his blockade – possibly even producing a prime – but to do this he will have to bring builders into his outerboard. If your back men are split, they are a source of danger to him as you have two points from which to hit and he may even leave you a direct shot. Then your next step will be to use any high rolls you may have to run with the back men. An alternative method (if you can't play the first) is for you to try to develop a blocking strategy as well. If neither of these work then your last resort is to play a back game.

Let's look at a few examples to make these points clear. (See Diagram 139.)

Black has to play 6–2. Looking at the board there is only one way for him to move. Red has managed to produce half a prime and is aiming to make his 5-point, thereby forming a blockade of four points; he has also managed to escape with his two back men, so Black must move one of his back men all the way to Red's 9-point, as in Diagram 140.

BLACK HOME

RED HOME

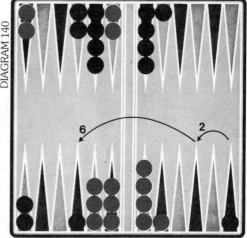

6   2

In Diagram 141 Red has to play 3–2. Here Black has managed to make his 5-point, so his next step is to make his bar-point to produce a blockade covering four points. To counteract this Red must play his roll of 3–2 so as to combine running and blocking at the same time (Diagram 142).

In Diagram 143 Red has the chance to run with 6–4 but a much better play is to make his 4-point (as was done in the actual game). This is a blocking versus blocking strategy – check for yourself from Diagram 144 why this is a better move than a running one would be.

In the next example, Diagram 145, Black has to play 1–1. At first glance it's very tempting to make his bar-point, producing half a prime. In fact that would be perfectly correct play had Red's men still been right at the back. Since Red has advanced his back men though, Black must cancel Red's advantage by moving his back men (as he did in the actual game) all the way (Diagram 146).

Try to remember, always look for the opportunity of avoiding being blocked; the timing factor is vital.

SECTION C. HOW TO PLAY AGAINST A BACK GAME

The defence against a back game is really the reverse of what we said in Chapter V, Section C (The Strategy of the Back Game).

If your opponent has adopted a back game strategy he will first try to establish himself in your homeboard. In order to do this he will probably leave as many blots as possible. It may be tempting for you to hit, but your first priority is to make points in, or near (i.e. the bar-point) your homeboard – as many and as quickly as you can. Only when you have a good board (four or five points) may you permit yourself the luxury of hitting, because then your opponent will have to pile most of his back men on one point which will not give him a proper back game. So – don't help him to slow down: that's exactly what he wants. Remember, the success of his back game depends first and foremost on how much help you give him to establish it!

In Diagram 147 Red has to play 6–3.

If he uses the 6 to hit Black on his own bar-point as shown in Diagram 148 then he is playing right into Black's hands. Black has already made two points in Red's homeboard, and all he now needs is time to build his own board. Why should Red help him? Red has a much better play to make. Look at Diagram 149.

Although Red is leaving a blot the play is correct. It is too early for Black to hit so Red is taking

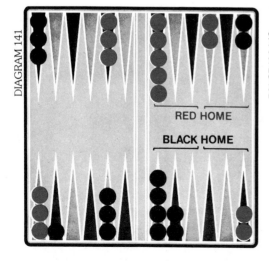

RED HOME

BLACK HOME

DIAGRAM 141

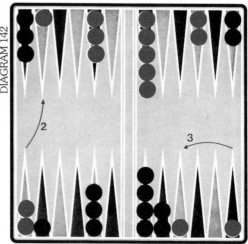

DIAGRAM 142

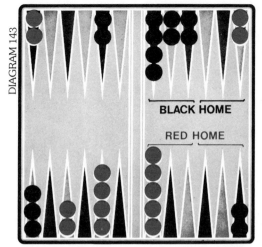

DIAGRAM 143

BLACK HOME

RED HOME

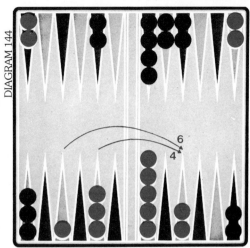

DIAGRAM 144

6
4

DIAGRAM 145

RED HOME

BLACK HOME

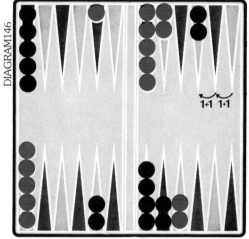

DIAGRAM 146

1+1 1+1

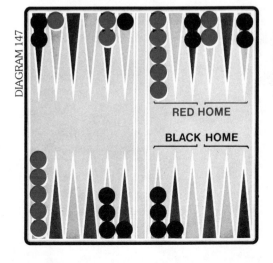

DIAGRAM 147

RED HOME

BLACK HOME

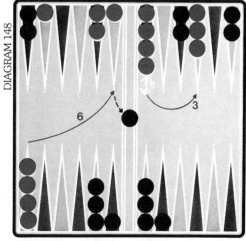

DIAGRAM 148

6
3

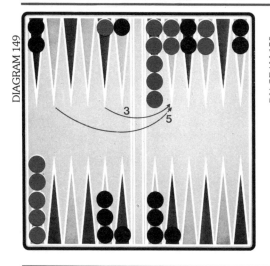

DIAGRAM 149

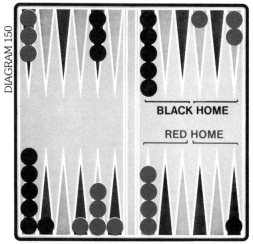

DIAGRAM 150

BLACK HOME

RED HOME

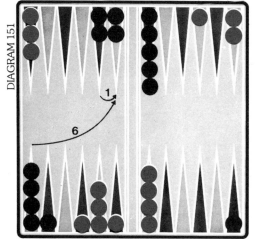

DIAGRAM 151

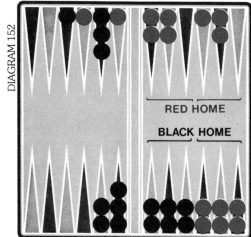

DIAGRAM 152

RED HOME

BLACK HOME

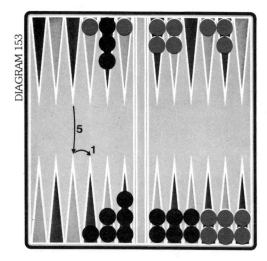

DIAGRAM 153

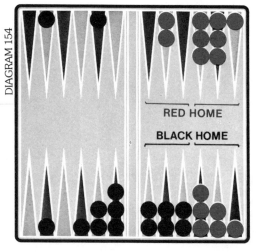

DIAGRAM 154

RED HOME

BLACK HOME

advantage of this to build points in his homeboard as quickly as possible.

In Diagram 150 Black has to play 6–1.

With this roll, he could run with his back man, hitting at the same time, and then also save his blot in Red's outerboard. Once again though, this is helping his opponent, for Red could then establish two points in Black's homeboard without having to develop his own game at all. What Black must do at this stage is concentrate on a blocking strategy by making his bar-point (Diagram 151).

It's true that Black has left two blots, but the position gained by the play – half a prime blocking three of Red's men – is worth the risk.

In Diagram 152 Black has to play 5–1. Looking at Red's position it can be seen that he is very well placed for a back game, but there is a hitch. He is moving much too fast. What he needs now is the 'help' of his opponent to put him on the bar. Once there, he may be able to maintain his good back game position; and if he doesn't have this chance (his only chance) of slowing himself down, then he will very soon have to break his board – should he manage to build it at all. In any case he will certainly have to move down from the highest points so that even if he does have a shot at Black later on, it probably won't help him to win. So for Black to hit Red's blot would be a big mistake. His correct move is to prepare to build a prime, should it be necessary. See Diagram 153.

Now Red is able to play any roll he might throw – a situation he does not particularly want. A few rolls later (Red having rolled an unpleasant 4–4, to which Black replied with 6–3, and then Red with 3–2) the position looked like Diagram 154, with Black to play 3–2.

It is very tempting now for Black to produce his prime using the 2; how the 3 is played then becomes irrelevant. Let's look for a moment at the situation that that would produce (Diagram 155).

What, you may ask, could be better than producing a prime and blocking six men at the same time? But don't forget – there is another stage of the game that has yet to take place, the bearing off process. And *now* is the time for Black to be thinking about it. If Black decides to produce his prime, then all Red can do is continue making his already very fast board even faster. Meanwhile, Black, maintaining the prime as long as possible to keep Red blocked, will be forced to pile most of his men on the highest points in his homeboard. Then sooner or later Black will have to break the prime, Red will start coming out, and long shots will be more to his advantage than to Black's. Also, from Red's point of view the fewer rolls he can play at this stage the better: so for Black to build a prime now would merely be helping Red. In the actual game

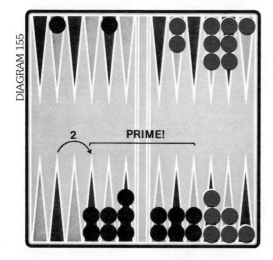

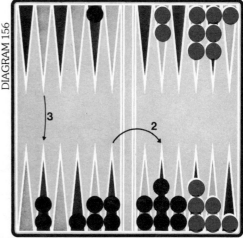

(The World Cup Tournament USA v UK, held at the Clermont in October 1974) the roll was played as shown in Diagram 156.

Black is trying to force Red to play a 6 and thus weaken his position in Black's homeboard. (Double 6 could now be disastrous for Red – check for yourself.) So Black's main aim is to force Red to break the 3-point. In this move, in fact, is the secret of how to defend yourself against a good back game. When your opponent is in the back game position, you must force him to play in such a way that he weakens himself both in your homeboard and in his, i.e. by breaking up his board. If you can do so, you may be able to relieve yourself of many of the problems that could otherwise occur at the end of the game when you are in the process of bearing off. Remember once again – the time factor is vital to your opponent. Don't help him!

VII

General Strategy

In my opinion the secret of backgammon is the '5–5 philosophy'. By this I mean that *the player who controls both the 5-points on the board controls the game.* It follows that if your opponent has managed to make your 5-point, then immediately try to make his. (This also applies to the bar-points.) That is why it is so important to come to a 'position' as quickly as possible and why, sometimes, one has to take a controlled risk to do so – hence some of the opening moves where a man was dropped on to the 5-point.

A description of general strategy falls naturally into three parts – strategy at the beginning of the game, in the middle, and at the end, so we shall take each part in turn.

SECTION A. STRATEGY AT THE BEGINNING OF THE GAME

We saw earlier that the main objective at the beginning of the game is to try to come to a position as quickly as possible, so we shall deal here with four different situations that can arise at this stage.

1. *Making your 5-point or hitting*

In Diagram 157 Black has to play 3–1. He could hit Red's blot, but it is obviously a much better strategy to make his own 5-point as shown in Diagram 158. It's true that Red may in turn make his 5-point on his next roll, but what is important is that Black has managed to come to a position first.

In Diagram 159 Black again has to play 3–1, and again he has the chance of hitting Red. But if he does hit (on the bar-point) he can't cover his blot with this roll – providing Red with 16/36 chances of a return shot. So Black could find himself back at the beginning of the game – and with three men. So again it is much better for Black to make his 5-point, as shown in Diagram 160. As before, Black is gaining position.

In Diagram 161 Black has to play 5–1. Let's assume he decides to hit, as shown in diagram 162. Now Red has 15/36 chances of hitting back, and with his good board this could mean disaster for Black. But if Black plays as shown in Diagram 163, he is coming to a position; and that, coupled with the fact that he already controls Red's bar-point and has a fair chance of making his own as well, could put him in a very strong blocking position.

In Diagram 164 Black again has to play 5–1 – and is faced with a very difficult decision indeed! He has two choices open to him. He can either play by hitting Red as in Diagram 165, in which case Red now has 24/36 chances of hitting Black (2 to 1 in Red's favour); only four rolls (6–4, 6–6, 4–4) will actually keep him on the bar. (While 5–4, 4–3, 4–2, 4–1 are not 'good' rolls for

DIAGRAM 157

RED HOME

BLACK HOME

DIAGRAM 158

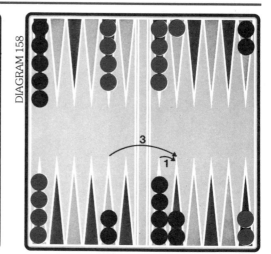

DIAGRAM 159

BLACK HOME

RED HOME

DIAGRAM 160

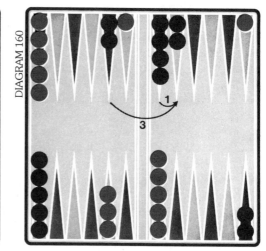

DIAGRAM 161

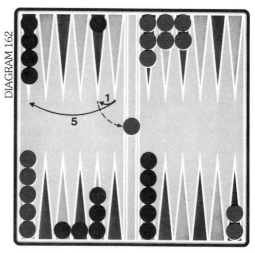

RED HOME

BLACK HOME

DIAGRAM 162

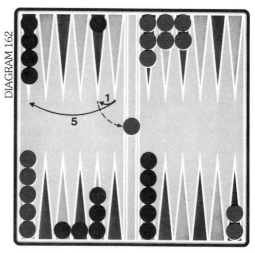

Red, they are playable.) So Black could find himself in deep water despite the fact that Red has three men at the back. Black's aim with this move was to prevent Red blocking him, but if he played as in Diagram 166 (as he did in the actual game), then Black is moving into a blocking position. While Red may make his bar-point to block Black, Black still has a good chance himself of making his own bar-point, which would give him an even better block. Add to that the fact that Black will have more freedom of movement for his back men than Red, and you can see why this is the better play.

2. Making a point other than the 5-point, or running and hitting

In Diagram 167 Red has to play 5–3. He could make a point in his homeboard, but the correct play here is to hit Black's blot as shown in Diagram 168. Red has not only managed to start running with one of his back men but he has forced Black back to the beginning with three men. The principle to remember here is that presented with the opportunity of making a point in your homeboard (other than the 5-point), or of running with a back man who can also hit – then run and hit!

DIAGRAM 163

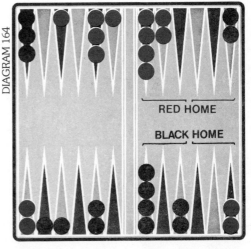

DIAGRAM 164

RED HOME

BLACK HOME

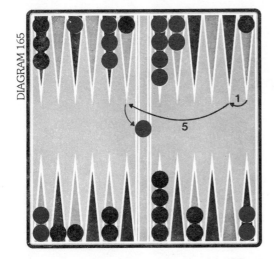

DIAGRAM 165

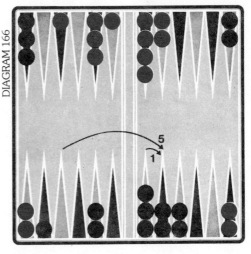

DIAGRAM 166

3. Hitting a blot in your homeboard

Red has rolled 6–6 in Diagram 169, and you can immediately see that he has a problem. He has a blot in his homeboard which cannot be covered, but he must hit Black to try to stop Black hitting him. He also wants to halt Black's movement temporarily so that he has time to save the blots that he must leave. For if he is going to hit Black on the 1-point he must also cover his 2-point in order to make Black's entry from the bar as difficult as possible. So the position now looks like Diagram 170. The real danger for Red lies in the rolls 5–3 and 5–2, both of which would enable Black to hit twice.

In Diagram 171 Red has to play 4–3. Black has managed to produce half a prime by making his bar-point, and had this been his move he could run with at least one of his back men – so Red's concern now is to stop Black enlarging his blockade. The only way he can do that is by making his 5-point with the 3, and then hitting on his 2-point with the 4, as shown in Diagram 172. By putting Black on the bar, Red has ensured that part of Black's next roll will have to be used to re-enter and therefore he will not be able to increase the block to four points – unless he rolls a miracle 1–1 or 4–4. So the object here of hitting in your homeboard, even if you have to leave a blot there, is to stop your opponent temporarily from coming to a position, while at the same time giving yourself more opportunity to run with your back men.

4. Hitting twice

This strategy is probably the most powerful you can use at the beginning of the game. By putting two of your opponent's men on the bar you force him to use both throws of a regular roll to re-enter – and should he throw any 6 he will be able to come in with only one man. This gives you the chance to develop your position or strengthen it if you are particularly weak somewhere on the board.

Let's look at some examples. In Diagram 173 Black has to play 6–5. If he uses the roll to run with one of his back men, he will then give Red the chance to make either or both bar-points, thus giving Red control of the board. So Black *must* hit: first on the bar-point, and then in his homeboard. If he hits only on the bar-point then Red, with one man to come in, could enter and hit Black back. So it's vital that Black hits in both places, as shown in Diagram 174. If anything goes wrong he still holds Red's 1-point and thus has an anchor to which he can return.

In Diagram 175 Red has to play 4–1. He could save his blot in Black's outerboard with the 1, but then what about the 4? Whichever way he plays it, Black will be given the chance to

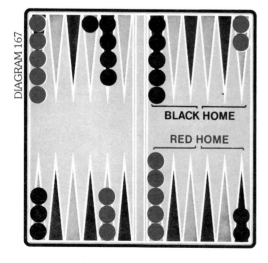

BLACK HOME

RED HOME

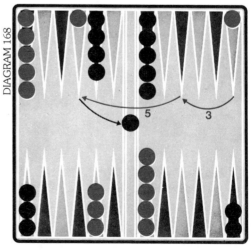

5

3

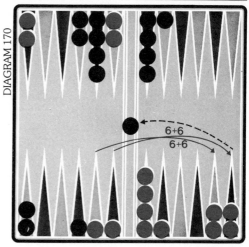

DIAGRAM 169

BLACK HOME

RED HOME

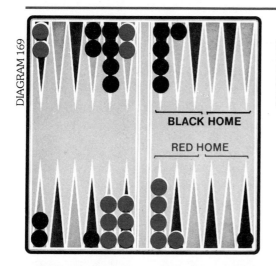

DIAGRAM 170

6+6

6+6

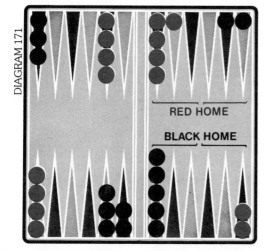

DIAGRAM 171

RED HOME

BLACK HOME

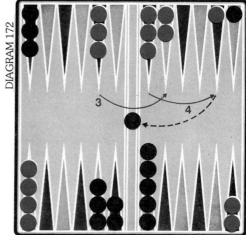

DIAGRAM 172

3

4

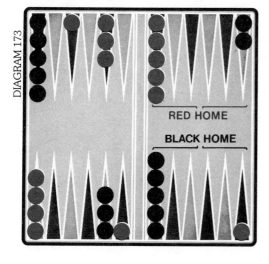

DIAGRAM 173

RED HOME

BLACK HOME

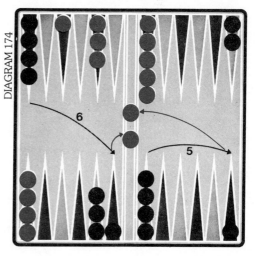

DIAGRAM 174

6

5

improve his position on either side of the board; so Red must use the 4 and the 1 to hit twice in his homeboard as shown in Diagram 176. Once again by hitting twice time is being gained to try to come to a position first.

Now (in Diagram 177) Red has to play 6–5. Well, he has to enter with the 5, thereby hitting. But now what does he do with the 6? Again, the best solution is to put another of Black's men on the bar, hitting on his (Red's) 2-point: see Diagram 178. As before, Red is trying to gain time by hitting twice.

In Diagram 179 Black has to play 5–4, and his problem is deciding what to do with the 4. The way Black played the roll in the actual game from which this example is taken was most unusual, and you can benefit enormously by studying the move very carefully: look at Diagram 180. First of all remember that Black has an anchorage in Red's board in case he is hit. Now what are the chances of Red entering off the bar and hitting either one or both of Black's blots? With 4–1 – and only with 4–1 – Red can hit twice (2/36 chances); with 4–3, 4–2, 3–1, 2–1, 1–1, 2–2, or 4–4 Red can enter both men but only hit once (11/36 chances); with 6–4, 6–1, 5–4, 5–1, Red can only bring in one man but he does hit at the same time (8/36 chances); with 6–3, 6–2, 5–3, and 5–2 Red brings in one man and does not hit (8/36 chances); with 3–2 and 3–3 Red can bring both men in but cannot hit (3/36 chances), while with 6–5, 5–5, or 6–6 Red can't enter at all (4/36 chances). Remember in all these cases that it is Black to roll next. So Black has 15/36 chances of being able to play his full roll next time because he will not be hit at all; and in the 19/36 chances of him being hit once, it is still him to roll first – while there are only 2/36 chances that two men will be put on the bar. So it wasn't such wild play by Black after all!

SECTION B. STRATEGY IN THE MIDDLE OF THE GAME

We said previously that the strategy at the beginning of the game was to try to come to a position as quickly as possible, attempting to play one type of pure strategy or another. In the middle of the game the strategy becomes more complex since now is the time that you will have either to mix or to switch strategies. There are really six different components at this stage.

1. Hitting twice

The strategy of hitting twice, or hitting a second man when one is already on the bar, is mainly used at this stage of the game to help you bring the game under your control. To do so you will find that a second hit becomes essential. Let's look at some examples.

In Diagram 181 Red has to play 5–2. Checking Black's position we see that he has a man on the bar, with odds of 3 to 1 *on* that he will enter this man and be able to play; and he has managed to produce half a prime blocking six men, so that at this stage he is playing a combination of blocking and running strategies. Red, on the other hand, is in a much weaker position. He has six men at the back and had it been Black's turn now, he would more than likely have been able to make another point in his homeboard, blocking Red's men even further. So Red must put another of Black's men on the bar by hitting with the 5 on his 8-point. Now the odds are 3 to 1 *against* Black bringing in both men.

But how should Red play the 2? He could make his bar-point, producing half a prime and reducing the blots in his outerboard, which sounds quite sensible – he would then be developing a blocking strategy too. But in fact it would be a mistake. Firstly, Black with two men on the bar can only hit Red in his outerboard with a roll of 4–4; secondly, by playing like this Red is decreasing his chances of making an extra point in his homeboard on his next roll, should it be necessary; and thirdly, Red is not taking advantage of Black being on the bar to start moving out of his back game position. So the correct way of playing the 2 is to move the man on Black's 3-point up to the 5-point. Now he has an extra man to hit again without having to break this

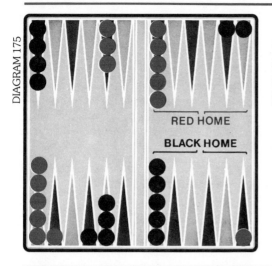

DIAGRAM 175

RED HOME

BLACK HOME

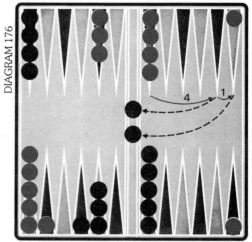

DIAGRAM 176

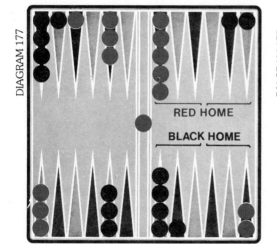

DIAGRAM 177

RED HOME

BLACK HOME

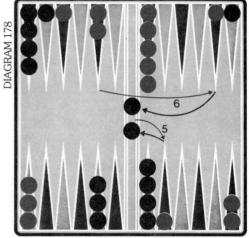

DIAGRAM 178

DIAGRAM 179

RED HOME

BLACK HOME

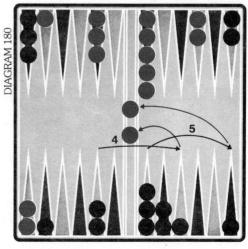

DIAGRAM 180

vital point, and he is reducing the blots in Black's homeboard. That's how the roll was played in the actual game (see Diagram 182).

Next look at Diagram 183. Here Black has rolled 6–1: how should he play it? You can see immediately that the problem is the 6. Black, in the actual game, played by hitting twice as in Diagram 184. But why? The blots in his outerboard can only be hit if Red rolls 4–4, and he not only has the safeguard of holding Red's 4-point but, should he be hit, might even be able to hit back on Red's blot! In fact Black is attempting to force Red to switch his strategy of partial running and blocking to a back game, because then Black will be in a very strong position to develop a proper blocking game.

In the next diagram (185) Red has to play 6–3. Now Black has a man on the bar that might hit Red's blot. So, if Red wants to play safe, he may move the man on his 11-point all the way to cover the blot. But he still leaves a blot on his 8-point and – more important – he has not improved his position one iota. He has another, and better, play open to him, as shown in Diagram 186. Let's analyse this play. Despite the fact that he still leaves a blot in his homeboard, Red has made another point and strengthened his position slightly; so it is an improvement on

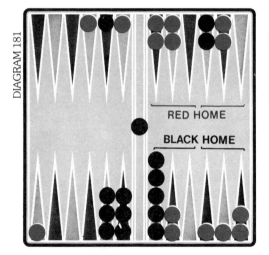

DIAGRAM 181

RED HOME

BLACK HOME

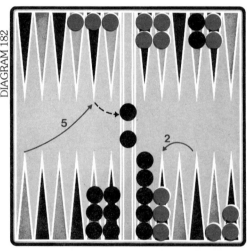

DIAGRAM 182

5

2

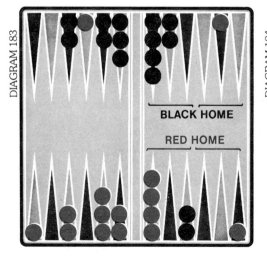

DIAGRAM 183

BLACK HOME

RED HOME

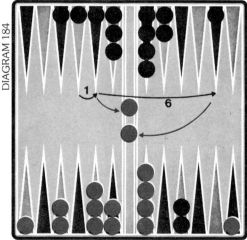

DIAGRAM 184

1

6

the previous play but it's not good enough. In both Diagrams 185 and 186 Red is blatantly ignoring one fundamental fact: he has four men at the back. And with one Black man on the bar already, it is the time for Red to attack. He can only attack in one way – by hitting again, as demonstrated in Diagram 187.

Now Black has two men on the bar meaning that Red is starting to gain control of the game; Red has also begun to come out of his back position, though still has an anchor should anything go wrong. Things will only go seriously wrong should Black roll 2–2, 3–3, or 5–5 (3/36 chances), as only with these rolls can Black enter both men *and* play. So any 2 for Black is not really dangerous for Red as, even if hit, Black may not get both men in; or if he does, he is not able to improve his position any further until the next roll. This is very dynamic play by Red, combining two main objectives – coming out of the back position and attacking at the same time. Always keep an eye open for this kind of combination: it's a policy that will pay.

In Diagram 188, Red has to play 3–1. He must use the 1 to enter on Black's 1-point – hitting at the same time – but the 3 is a problem. Let's just look at Diagram 189, after Red has entered off the bar. Assume for a moment that Red played the 3 from his 6-point to his 3-point

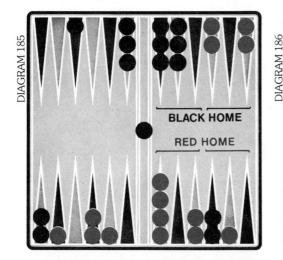

BLACK HOME

RED HOME

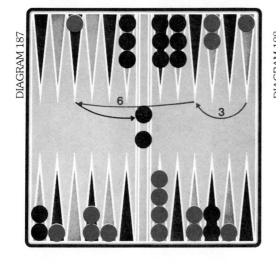

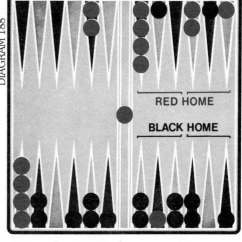

RED HOME

BLACK HOME

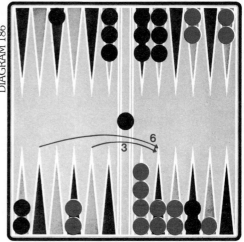

so as not to increase the number of blots he has on the board. Now only 6–3, 3–3, and 6–6 are bad rolls for Black, i.e. he will not be able to enter (4/36 chances). With 6–5, 6–4, 6–2, 6–1, 5–4, 5–3, 5–2, 5–1, 4–3, 4–2, 3–2, and 5–5 Black can enter, hitting once (23/36 chances), and with 4–1, 3–1, 2–1, 1–1, 2–2, and 4–4 Black can enter and hit twice (9/36 chances). Red will then have odds of 3 to 1 against bringing both men in with one roll – and will therefore lose control of the game. But if Red plays as shown in Diagram 190, using the 3 to hit again on his 5-point, then Black still can't enter with 6–3, 3–3, and 6–6 (4/36 chances); with 4–2 he can bring in both men without hitting (2/36 chances), and with 6–4, 6–2, 4–3, 3–2 he can only bring in one man who cannot hit (8/36 chances). This, so far, gives 14/36 chances of Black playing without hitting Red. Now with 6–5, 6–1, 5–3, 3–1 Black can only bring in one man but he does hit in doing so (8/36 chances); and with 5–4, 5–2, 4–1, 2–1, and 2–2 he enters both men hitting with one (9/36 chances). Altogether this gives 17/36 chances of Red being hit once (six chances less than the previous play) but he still has plenty of opportunity of entering and playing on his next roll. So only with 5–1, 1–1, 4–4, and 5–5 can Black enter both men and hit Red twice (5/36 chances – four fewer than before). Thus it is sometimes necessary to hit twice even if it means leaving two blots in the homeboard – and this in fact was what Red did in the actual game.

Now look at Diagram 191, where Red has to play 4–3. Once again there is no choice about the 3: he must use it to enter, obviously hitting at the same time. The 4 is not such a difficult decision here. Since Red has an anchor in Black's homeboard, he uses the 4 to hit again on his own 5-point, leaving only one blot in his homeboard as in Diagram 192.

It would be good practice, and very helpful to you, to work out this example for yourself on your board, and also the example shown in Diagram 188.

In Diagram 193 Black has to play 6–4. He has a very strong position so Red's only chance of getting back into the game is to make Black's 1-point. If it were Red's roll any 1 would enable him to do this (11/36 chances), so Black must use the 6 to hit from the bar-point. The only way Red can now make Black's 1-point is by rolling 1–1 (35 to 1 against) and with two men on the bar, he has only 4/36 chances of entering both men in one roll. Black therefore has no need of the bar-point at this stage. Should Red fail to roll a 1 next time Black can use the blot on his bar-point to cover the 1-point with any 6, excluding 2–2 (16/36 chances). He used the 4 to start moving from Red's bar-point so that if he needs to re-make his own, he still has a good chance of doing so. See Diagram 194.

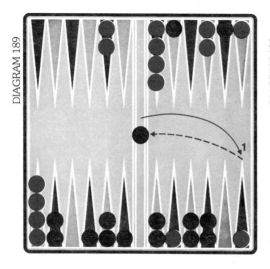

DIAGRAM 189

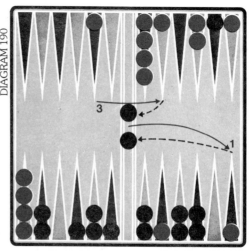

DIAGRAM 190

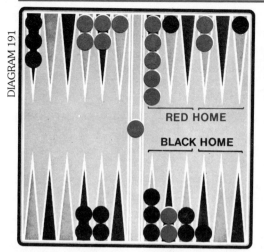

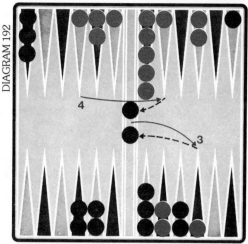

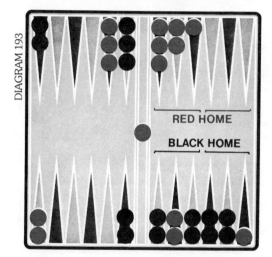

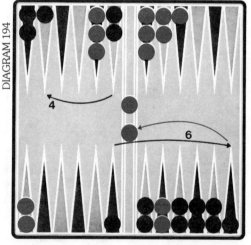

In Diagram 195 Black has rolled 3–3 – an excellent throw. With it he must change the game completely. At the moment both players are involved in back game and blocking strategies but Black now has the advantage, because of his very good roll, plus the fact that Red has a man on the bar. So the first thing Black must do is hit again, making his 4-point at the same time, as shown in Diagram 196. Now, with two men on the bar Red is 8 to 1 against entering both in one roll (only 2–1, 1–1, and 2–2 will enable him to do this), so Black has time to start moving out of his back position. But first he must ask himself what Red really wants to do now; and the answer to that is quite clear. If Red can roll any 1 (11/36 chances) he will then be able to make Black's 1-point – and once he holds that he will then have a perfect back game position, with timing to match! So if Black carries on moving his two men from the 4-point to the 1-point, as in Diagram 197, he not only prevents this but also changes the situation entirely.

Red now has three men on the bar, and only with 4–4 can he enter and play (hitting). The odds against him throwing double 4 are 35 to 1. Even if he manages to make Black's 4-point, still he will not have a proper back game. So Black has gained control, and has time to come out with his back men.

You can see from this how important it can be to prevent your opponent establishing himself on your 1-point if he is involved in a back game situation. So remember, hitting twice in the middle of the game, if properly done, can completely swing the balance of the game; and from the opposite point of view, be cautious about leaving too many blots!

2. Hitting process

Hitting in this instance is used mainly when a player needs extra time, either to relieve his back men or to improve his blocking position. It may lead (if it works) to a switch in strategy or to a strengthened board. To take an example, look at Diagram 198. Here Red has to play 4–4, and, having three men right at the back, is in real trouble. His immediate need is time to escape from Black's homeboard – and Black's blockade of five points is virtually as strong as a prime. Only a 6–2 or 6–1 will enable one of Red's back men to move out. So with his 4–4 Red must hit Black and at the same time decrease the latter's chances of re-entering. The only way to do so is by playing as shown in Diagram 199. Red has moved one man all the way from his 13-point to cover the blot on his 1-point, while with the extra man on the 6-point he hits Black's blot on the

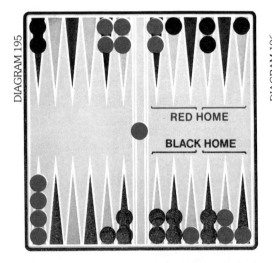

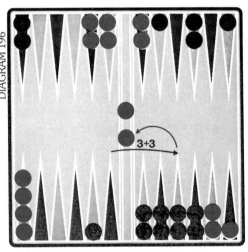

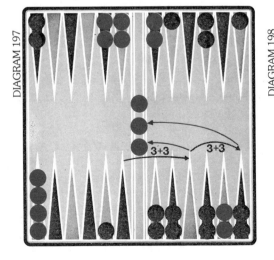

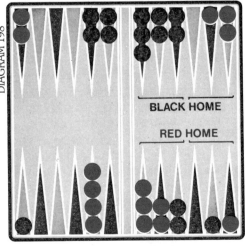

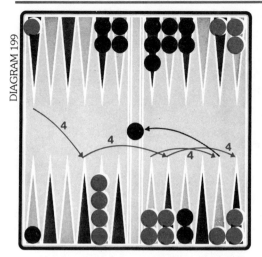

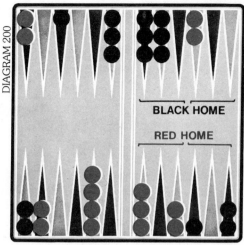

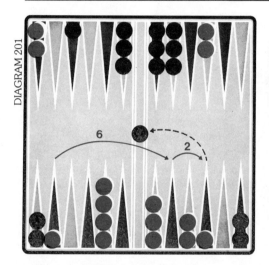

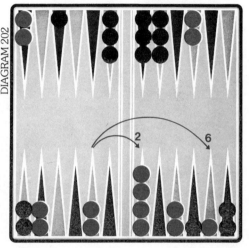

2-point. Thus he has managed to hit and make a third point in his homeboard simultaneously. This is a crucial moment for Red. If he is not hit then he may have a chance to move his back men out; if he is hit, even though he doesn't particularly want to be, he still has the alternative of a good back game position when being hit may help him to slow down.

In Diagram 200 Red has to play 6–2; you can see immediately that there is no way for him to play safe. Furthermore, he must not come out with one of his back men as this could lead to complete disaster. So he has two choices: one to hit on his 3-point as in Diagram 201, which gives Black 19/36 chances (6–5, 6–3, 5–3, 5–2, 4–3, 3–2, 3–1, 2–1, 1–1, 2–2, 3–3) to hit Red in return – who will then be blocked with three men at the back which will probably lose him the game. But should Red choose the other alternative and play as in Diagram 202, then Black can only hit with a 1 (11/36 chances). However it may not be convenient for him to hit with any 1; for 6–1, 3–1, and 2–1 (6/36 chances – more than 50% of his chances of hitting) will force him to decide between hitting or making his own 4-point, so as to produce a blockade of four points for Red's two men to overcome, and then hoping he will have another opportunity to hit the blot on Red's 2-point. So here it is not advisable to hit, the preferable move being as in Diagram 202.

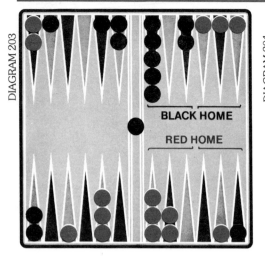

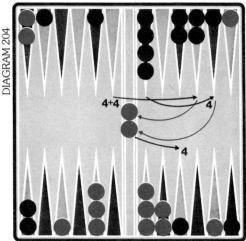

3. Breaking your bar-point to hit

In order to have a strong blocking position against a back game it is essential to have, if not the 5-point, the bar-point. The question is, how long should one keep it? Let's look at a few examples which illustrate the answer.

In Diagram 203 Black has to play 4–4. Firstly he must of course enter off the bar, but he is still left with three more 4s to play. Though Black has too many blots on the board, to play defensively here would be quite wrong. He must use this roll to its maximum effect to maintain control of the game. Taking into account that Red doesn't have a very good board and even has a blot there, leads Black to play as shown in Diagram 204. In fact this is the only good play he has.

Red now has two men on the bar and is 3 to 1 against bringing them both in with one roll, and even if Black is hit on his 2-point he may then retaliate on Red's 2-point. Black is controlling the board, plus the timing, in that he has made an extra point in his homeboard and may even be able to hit again. Any play that kept the bar-point intact at this stage would not be to his advantage.

Now look at Diagram 205. Here Black has to play 2–1. In the actual game this roll was played as shown in Diagram 206, so let's deal with this play first. The advantages of it are that Black has made his 5-point hitting at the same time, and now has a strong blockade against four of Red's men. And, if he is not hit, he may soon bring his last two men round to safety. But – therein lies the disadvantage: Red currently on the bar may, with 6–1, 6–2, 5–2, and 5–1, enter and then hit on Black's bar-point (8/36 chances). It's true that Red does not have an ideal board but still, five points are blocked and unless Black enters immediately (with any 6, 11/36 chances) Red may hit again (with a 9) the blot on Red's 9-point. If that happens Black will almost certainly lose control of the game. So here is an alternative way to play the roll: see Diagram 207.

Again Black has hit and made a point but now he cannot be hit in return! And, unlike the previous play, Red will not be able to establish a good back game position even if he manages to make Black's 5-point. (Holding the 1- and 5-points is not effective for a good back game.) In any case Red is much too fast, and also if Red can't make Black's 5-point, Black still has another chance of making it himself. So you must always consider very carefully whether or not it is worth breaking the bar-point to make the 5-point.

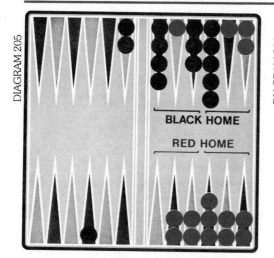

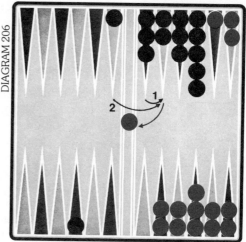

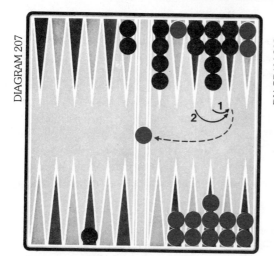

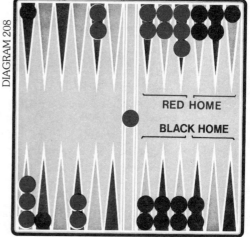

4. Coming out with the back men

The idea here is to switch from a back game, or partial back game, to a running strategy, while at the same time forcing your opponent into a back game, or at least holding him back as long as possible. To illustrate: in Diagram 208 Black has to play 5–4. Checking his position, though he has five men at the back he has a good board and Red is on the bar. This gives him the unexpected opportunity to stop Red (temporarily) from blocking him, by making Red's bar-point: see Diagram 209. Black will only have real problems now should Red roll 1–1 or 2–2, either of which would enable him to hit Black twice in the outerboards (2/36 chances). With 4–2, 4–1, and 2–1 Red can enter and hit once (6/36 chances) and with 6–2, 6–1, 5–2, 5–1, 3–2, and 3–1 (8/36 chances) he can enter, but otherwise the rolls are no help to him at all (check for yourself why not). With the remaining 16/36 chances, Red cannot get in. So Black's possession of Red's bar-point gives him quite good security.

Now in Diagram 210 Black has to play 6–4. Here he is in a very strong blocking position so he can take advantage of it and come out with both back men as shown in Diagram 211. He is now playing against any 1 (11/36 chances), though in fact not all 1s will be good for Red – he still has a blot in Black's homeboard so only 4–1 or 6–1 would enable him to hit and cover the blot. Also the 6–1 would be better used by coming out with the back man, who would of course have to hit.

5. Playing to close your board

Here the main objective is either to close your board while your opponent is on the bar or to produce a prime to block him. But in attempting to do so you must always remember that dropping a blot contains a high risk element – so make sure that you have the security of holding a point in your opponent's homeboard in case your plan goes wrong!

In Diagram 212 Black has to play 5–4. Looking at the board we can see that both players are blocked but Red has more men available for long shots so he has the better timing. Now Black could play safe by moving to his 9-point with the 4, leaving him vulnerable only to 5–3 from Red, and then play the 5 from his 8-point to the 3-point. But if he has to leave a blot somewhere – which he must – he ought to leave the man in such a position that if it is not hit, he can then use it to produce a prime to block Red's back men. He can do this if he plays as in Diagram 213. If the blot is hit (and not every 3 is really good for Red) then being put on the bar may help either to maintain his good blockade or to produce a back game. He really has no option but to make this move.

In the example in Diagram 214 Red has to play 4–3, which at first glance looks like the perfect roll. Red can make Black's 5-point with the 4 and his own bar-point with the 3. He leaves no blots and everything looks fine. But (there is always a 'but') he has an opportunity here to go for a gammon – and he should take it. If he plays the 4 as before, and it is a *must* to make Black's 5-point because only then can Red take a controlled risk, he can then drop a man on his 4-point with the 3, so his board looks like Diagram 215. The real danger here lies in Black rolling 6–4, for he would then hit twice. If Black fails to roll a 4 (11/36 chances) then Red has 25/36 chances of closing his board (any 1, any 6, and – with double 4s – 16) and he will then very probably win a gammon. This example might give you some ideas on whether to try for a gammon or to play safe, waiting hopefully for some new development that may never come!

6. Making use of a prime

The situation may arise where you have managed to produce a prime, blocking your opponent, and you now want to take advantage of your position: firstly to try to collect another of your

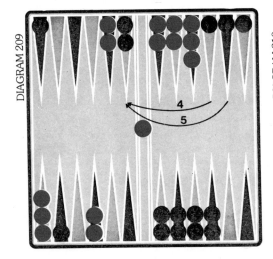

DIAGRAM 209

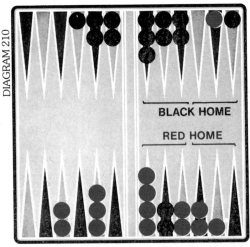

DIAGRAM 210

BLACK HOME

RED HOME

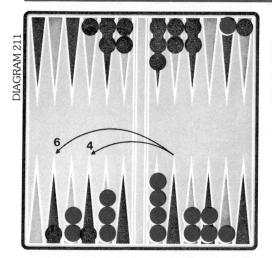

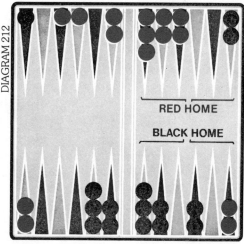

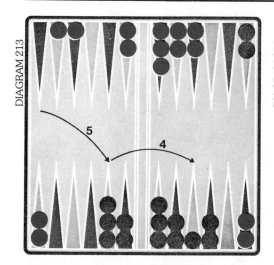

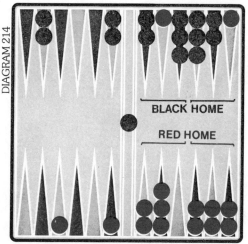

opponent's men, and secondly to gain time in anticipation of his board collapsing.

In Diagram 216 Black has to play 5–2, and there is only one way to play it: see Diagram 217. Black deliberately leaves a blot in Red's homeboard, because should Red now roll 6–5, 3–3, 5–5, or 6–6 he will in turn be forced to leave a blot. Even if Black doesn't hit first time round he will probably have another shot later. So always be on the watch for opportunities that may increase your chances of winning not only a gammon, but maybe even a backgammon.

SECTION C.   STRATEGY AT THE END OF THE GAME

In dealing with this section we must bear in mind that the end of the game does not necessarily mean the last roll. The end can start a few rolls before the final one. However we can distinguish between:

a) Ending the game in one roll. We have already looked (in Chapter I, sections 3 and 4) at the probabilities of bearing off the last one or two men in one roll. Always look before you move to see how to improve your chances of winning on the last roll. In Chapter IV we saw in some detail how to achieve this goal.

b) A few rolls before the last one a short cut may be needed to try to swing the game in your favour before it's too late. Let's look at some examples to illustrate this very vital point: first take a look at Diagram 218. Black has to play 4–2. He can play safe by moving his blot along four points and using a man from the 6-point to play the 2. Then Red on his next roll will be forced to leave a blot with 6–5, 6–4, 4–3, 5–5, and 6–6 (8/36 chances). But if Black played as in Diagram 219, then again 6–5, 6–4, 4–3, 5–5, and 6–6 will force Red to leave a blot (8/36 chances) but so will another roll: 4–4. This means that Red now has 9/36 chances of leaving a blot, and Black has two points from which he may hit – which is why he must play the roll in this way.

In Diagram 220 Red has to play 2–1: he must choose between playing safe and hitting. If he decides to play safe by breaking his bar-point (moving one man to his 6-point and one to his 5) then it's true that for the time being he is safe. But with any 6 (excluding doubles) he will have to leave two blots (10/36 chances) and with 5–2, 4–2, and 3–3 he will have to leave one blot (5/36 chances) – giving a total of 15/36 chances of at least one blot being left on his next roll. Black, with his good board, will then quite probably win the game, so Red *must* hit. But he must hit in such a way that he minimises the chances of his being hit in return. He has two different

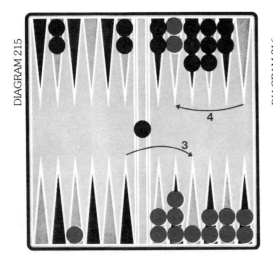

DIAGRAM 215

DIAGRAM 216

BLACK HOME

RED HOME

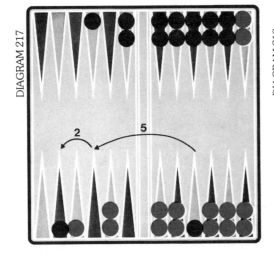

DIAGRAM 217

DIAGRAM 218

BLACK HOME

RED HOME

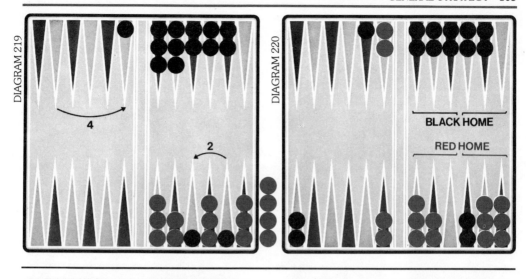

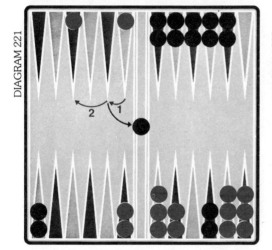

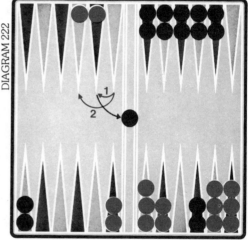

methods of play, the first as shown in Diagram 221. Now Black can enter with 6–4, 6–3, and 4–3 and hit once in the outerboard (6/36 chances); but with 3–3 he can enter and hit twice, giving a total of 7/36 chances for Red to be hit. The second play, as in Diagram 222, gives Black the same number of chances of entering and hitting (5–4, 5–3, 4–3, and 4–4) but he can only hit *once* with each roll. This is therefore the correct play for Red.

In Diagram 223 Black has to play 3–3. If you check the pip count before moving this roll, Black is 107 while Red is 68. So the roll of double 3 is not enough to close the gap, and there is worse to come. Black cannot hit the blot in Red's homeboard and it would be a great mistake to hit the blot in his own homeboard to make the 1-point. His one chance of winning is to keep Red's blot firmly blocked; at the moment Red can only come out with 6–2 (2/36 chances) whereas if he were on the bar 3–4, 3–5, and 3–6 would all enable him to enter and get out. So Black's only hope of increasing his chances for a single game is to 'give' Red as many opportunities as possible to leave a blot on his next roll. The only way in which he can do this is by playing as shown in Diagram 224.

Now if Red next rolls 6–5, 6–4, 6–3, 6–1, 5–4, 5–3, 5–1, 5–5, or 6–6, he will be forced to leave a blot (we are of course ignoring the blot in Black's homeboard for the moment). This gives a total of 16/36 chances for Black to have a shot so by moving as shown he is establishing control in the outerboard as well.

Now look at Diagram 225, where Red has rolled 6–2; it is instantly obvious that it is a difficult roll. In the actual game it took Red nearly five minutes to decide what to do. The choice is between hitting and not hitting. If he doesn't hit, then to keep the chance of his being hit himself to a minimum he must play as illustrated in Diagram 226. With this play Black may now hit with any 6 (excluding 2–2) (16/36 chances); he could, with 6–4, hit twice and in any event may have another shot later in his outerboard.

The roll in the actual game was in fact played as shown in Diagram 227 – Red hit twice! With this play he has brought the game to its crucial moment. Let's look at what could happen now. Black with 6–2, 2–2, and 6–6 (4/36 chances) is not in at all; with 4–3 and 3–3 he brings in both men without hitting (3/36 chances); with 6–4, 6–3, 4–2, and 3–2 (8/36 chances) he can only bring in one man and cannot hit: so far we have 15/36 chances for Red to be in a position of playing any roll he may have. Black, with 6–1, 5–2, and 2–1 can only bring in one man but hits

BLACK HOME

RED HOME

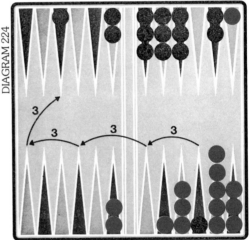

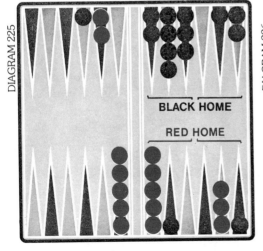

BLACK HOME

RED HOME

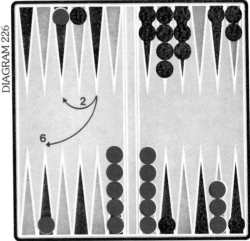

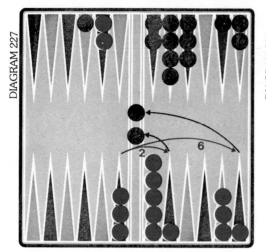

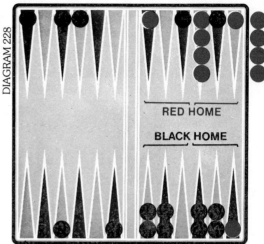

at the same time (6/36 chances); but Red could still play most rolls (16/36 chances) while Black is on the bar with his remaining man, and Red may hit again in Black's homeboard with a 2. With 5–4, 5–3, 4–1, 3–1, 4–4, and 5–5 Black can bring both men in and hit once at the same time (10/36 chances) which will put Red in the same position that we have just mentioned. Only with 5–1 (2/36 chances) can Black bring in both men and hit *twice*. So in the majority of cases (24/36 chances) Red has the advantage in timing. There are only 12/36 chances for Black to enter both men and hit at least once simultaneously, in which case Red will quite probably lose control of the game (although he may, as mentioned, hit the blot in Black's board). This is a very unusual example of how to bring the game to a climax by taking a controlled risk.

In Diagram 228 Red has to play 6–2. He is forced to play the 6 by hitting on Black's bar-point but what about the 2? At first glance it might look as though it should be played as in Diagram 229, to cover his 1-point and eliminate the number of blots – and of course Black is on the bar. With 3–1, 1–1, and 3–3 Black cannot enter (4/36 chances); with 4–1, 2–1, and 5–5 he is in but cannot hit (5/36 chances); with 6–5, 6–4, 6–2, 6–1, 5–4, 5–3, 5–2, 5–1, 4–3, 4–2, 3–2, and 2–2 he is in and hits once (23/36 chances); while with 6–3, 4–4, and 6–6 Black enters and hits twice, giving a total of 27/36 chances for Black to hit at least once. With his good homeboard and control of the rest of the board he may hit yet again and win. So what else could Red do? Here (Diagram 230) is how the roll was played in the actual game from which the example is taken, when Red decided to hit twice. With 3–3 Black is not in (1/36 chances); with 6–5, 6–2, 5–2, and 5–5 he can enter both men but cannot hit (7/36 chances); with 6–3, 5–3, and 3–2 he can bring in only one man without hitting (6/36 chances), so far giving Red 14/36 chances to play any roll – five chances more than he had before. With 4–3 and 3–1 Black can bring in only one man but hits at the same time (4/36 chances); with 6–4, 6–1, 5–4, 5–1, 4–2, 2–1, 1–1, 2–2, and 6–6 he can bring both men in and hit once (15/36 chances) while with 4–1 and 4–4 he can enter the two men and hit twice (3/36 chances, one less than the previous play). So in total Black has 22/36 chances of hitting at least once, which is five chances fewer than in the previous play shown in Diagram 229. Therefore Red must play the odds, as he did in the game.

In Diagram 231 Black has to play 5–1. His choice is between running with one of the back men or sitting tight. Either way Red needs at most three rolls to finish the game (he might bear off only one man on his next roll, then either one or two, and then the last one or two remaining men with the third roll), and assuming that Black fails to hit (Red's only chance of winning a gammon or backgammon) then Black will need on his next two rolls double 6s, or double 6 and double 5

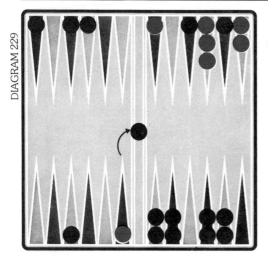

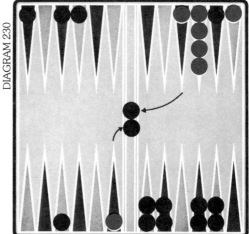

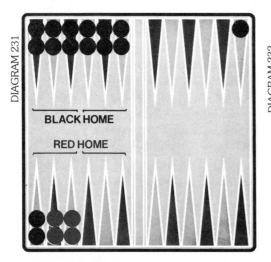

BLACK HOME

RED HOME

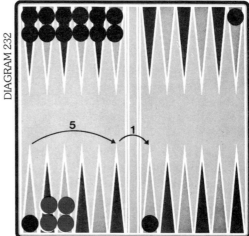

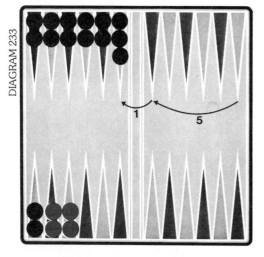

consecutively – 1296 to 1 against! So Black must check whether or not he can increase his chances of hitting, and if so, how? If he runs as shown in Diagram 232, then Red will be forced to leave one blot with 6–2, 5–2, 4–2, 3–2, 2–1 (10/36 chances) which will give Black 11/36 chances to hit back. If on the other hand Black stays put as in Diagram 233, then Red will be forced to leave one blot with 2–1 (2/36 chances), but with 6–2, 5–2, 4–2, and 3–2 will be forced to leave two blots (8/36 chances). Black will now have 20/36 chances to hit Red, nine more opportunities than previously. In both cases Red has ten bad shots. So if Black runs he is not improving his chances of saving a gammon, whereas if he stays he does increase his chances of hitting at least once and hence it is more likely that he will save himself a gammon – or even a backgammon.

VIII

The Doubling Process

SECTION A. WHAT IS THE DOUBLING PROCESS?

To make this – the most important aspect of backgammon – as clear as possible, we shall first define the meaning of the term according to the International Laws of Backgammon, then deal with the various other kinds of doubling that may be agreed between the two players, and lastly we shall discuss the mathematical aspects of the doubling process.

Firstly, though, what *is* the doubling process (according to International Law)? Before beginning to play the two players must agree on a 'unit': it can be £1, £2, £10 – anything so long as both are in agreement. The agreed unit is then known as *one original unit*. When the doubling process is in use this unit is multiplied according to the figure face up on the doubling cube.

How the doubling process works (also called 'regular doubling' or 'voluntary doubling')

At the beginning of the game the doubling cube is placed in the middle between the two players, either on the bar or on the left or right of the board, with the figure 64 face up and sideways on to each player. The fact that the 64 is face up does not mean that the game is starting at that figure – it starts at one original unit. The 64 is merely indicating at the beginning that the doubling cube has not yet come into force.

Each player is entitled to use the doubling cube for the first time at any stage of the game in the following way. Whoever decides to use it first must do so *before* he rolls the dice (reasons leading one to use the cube for the first time will be discussed later). Having decided that he wants to double, the player picks up the cube and places it near his opponent (on the left or right of the board) having turned it so that the figure 2 is now facing up, and says 'I double you'. If his opponent refuses to accept the double the game is over; and by refusing, that player loses just the one original unit. But if he accepts, the cube is left near him and – until the next double – he has the cube *under control*. The game then continues with a new unit equal to two original units, so that the player who wins it will score (for a single game) those two original units. The figure 2 on the cube is multiplied by the one original unit, i.e. if the original stake was £1, he will win 2 × £1 = £2. If he wins a gammon, then the score becomes four original units (the 2 on the cube multiplied by two original units), and if he wins a backgammon then he wins six original units (2 on the cube multiplied by three original units).

After the first double has been offered and accepted, the next double may only be offered by the player who has the cube under control. He may do so at any stage of the game, in the manner described before, by placing the cube near his opponent on either side of the board but this time with the figure 4 face up. If the player to whom the new double has been offered refuses it, then as before the game is over and he loses the new unit that was equal to two original units. If he accepts, *he* now has the cube under control (and is therefore entitled to offer the next double) and there is another new unit equal to four original units. Whoever wins the game scores four original units (4×1) for a single game; eight original units (4×2) for a double game (gammon); and twelve original units (4×3) for a triple game (backgammon). The next double offered, if accepted, will bring the new unit up to eight original units, and so on.

Described above is the technical side of the use of the doubling cube. From now on, however, we must bear in mind that it is an integral piece of the game's equipment, and not just an object lying beside the board. It is an instrument, or more appropriately we could call it a weapon, that moves with us from the first stage of the game. Properly used, the cube can increase the chances of winning higher stakes; while failure to master its proper use can lead to catastrophe. So we shall look at the doubling process from the mathematical point of view in some detail, but first let's just consider some other kinds of doubling.

Other kinds of doubling

All the doubling processes discussed below may take place only by agreement between the players and must be decided and agreed upon before the start of the game.

a) *Automatic Doubles.* These apply only at the beginning of the game when both players are rolling for the first opening move. If each player's die rolls the same number, then the doubling cube is automatically turned to 2 – but the cube remains *in the middle between the players*. If both players again roll the same number the cube is then turned to 4, and again remains where it is. It makes sense when agreeing to play automatic doubles to restrict them to just one or two, but this entirely depends on the agreement reached between yourself and your opponent. One can prevent automatic doubling by increasing the stake, again by prior agreement, to two units – whereupon the doubling cube is turned to 2 once again remaining in the middle between the two players. After automatic doubling has taken place, regular doubling may then occur during the game as usual.

b) *Optional Doubles.* These are extra starting doubles again agreed upon before starting the game. Each player rolls his one die and if automatic doubles have been agreed upon, then obviously they apply if the dice are the same. If however they are not the same, but the player who has rolled the highest number does not like his opening move, he may turn the cube one number higher than before, and roll again. The cube still remains in the middle of the board. The second player may also refuse his opening throw and turn the cube up one.

This option is allowed to both players on their first throws only. And note that in optional doubles, if either player rolls a double, then the cube is automatically turned up one again. After optional doubles, regular doubling may take place during the game as usual.

Do remember that if you do not wish to be involved in this type of double, eliminate it by agreement before you start the game or you may find yourself with the cube on a high number before play has even begun.

c) *Initial Double Dice.* Here each player starts by rolling two dice, and in this case a double roll counts its face value, i.e. 3–3 equals 6 and not 12. The player rolling the highest number (the sum of both dice) plays first and he may now use the optional double if he doesn't like his opening throw. His opponent of course has the same privilege. Do not forget that in playing this type of double, automatic doubles also apply; so if the total sum of both your dice equals that of your opponent's dice, then the doubling cube is again automatically turned to the next number.

Needless to say, prior agreement is vital. Regular doubling takes places normally during the game after the initial double.

d) *Beavers.* Here the player who has been offered a double has the right to redouble *immediately*, i.e. turn the cube to the next number up, and still retain 'control' of the cube. For instance, suppose that player A doubles, the cube is then placed near player B with the figure 2 face up. If player B accepts the double and wishes to beaver, he then turns the cube to 4 before player A rolls the dice, *and the cube stays on player B's side*. Player A may of course refuse the beaver if he wishes, and so on.

e) *Raccoons.* Again this must be agreed upon previously, and occurs when player A wishes to redouble after player B has beavered. (So, the original double to 2 offered by player A will now be 8.) Remember though, this type of double can be *exceedingly* hazardous! *(N.B. The cube stays on player B's side, although it was player A who redoubled last.)*

One more word about all these doubles: make sure that you have discussed and agreed upon any or all of them *before* you start playing and be especially cautious of people who offer you any of them without a limit attached.

The mathematical viewpoint

Let's assume that player A is offering the first double. His reasoning goes something like this: 'I think I have a better position than B' (and later we shall see what player A has to know in order to be sure that he has a better position) 'and I think I can win a single game, in which case I shall win one original unit (say, £1). However, I would like to increase this unit by at least one more. I could do this if the game were played at double the original stake. So I shall offer my opponent a double in the hope that he accepts and I can then take advantage of my good position to win the game, which of course means that I shall win double the original stake agreed at the beginning. It's a good proposition and it is therefore worthwhile offering B a double.'

Player B now says to himself: 'Player A has offered me a double because he has a better position than I have at this stage of the game. So far I haven't lost anything but if I refuse, the game is immediately over and I lose one unit (£1). On the other hand if I accept the double, the game continues and may develop in such a way that I end up losing a single game, in which case I shall be one unit worse off (£1) than if I had refused the double. But equally the game could develop so that I win a single game, in which case I'll win two units (£2) and be three times better off than if I'd refused the double. So: if I refuse the double immediately I definitely lose one unit (£1); if I accept it I may lose a single game of two units (£2) making me one unit (£1) worse off than my immediate refusal, but if I win a single game – which I might – then I win the two units (£2) and am three times better off than if I refuse now. Thus, if I accept the double I'm accepting a proposition of 3 to 1 to be better off. So, I think I shall accept it. But if I lose a gammon then I shall lose four units (£4) making me three times worse off than if I refused the double now. Well, to risk an extra unit (£1) just to lose three more (£3) is obviously not a good proposition. (It's not good because to risk an extra pound and possibly be gammoned, thereby losing £4, puts me in the position of losing £3 more than I would if I refused the double now, and gives me even odds of 3 to 3 either to double and win a single game or to double and lose a gammon.)

'Now before I make a final decision, what happens should I lose a backgammon? Well, I'd lose six units (£6), so by accepting the double I'm risking an extra unit (or an extra £1) to find myself worse off by five units (£5). That's no proposition as, even if I win a single game (which is by no means definite at this stage) the odds against me are still 3 to 5. So let me check that there is no danger of my losing a gammon or backgammon, in which case I shall accept the double. If there is a possibility that I might lose a double or even triple game then I shall have to refuse it – why lose more than one unit (£1) after all?'

This leads us to the fundamental law of the doubling process: *when the odds are more than 3 to 1 in your opponent's favour you must refuse if he offers you a double* – although no one can prevent you from losing money if you really want to! Let's analyse why you have to refuse the double if the odds are more than 3 to 1 against. If the game is played at a pound a point, odds of 3 to 1 mean then that your opponent expects to win seventy-five pence and to lose twenty-five pence, in other words he is expecting to win seventy-five minus twenty-five pence, which equals fifty pence. But if he doubles then he expects to win fifty pence multiplied by two, i.e. one pound, which is exactly what it will cost you to refuse the double. If the odds are more than 3 to 1 in your opponent's favour then he will expect to win more than a pound if he doubles, and of course what he is expecting to win is what you are going to lose. Let's say the odds are 4 to 1 in his favour and he offers a double: at these odds he expects to win eighty pence and lose twenty pence, in other words he expects a gain of eighty minus twenty pence, which equals sixty pence. If he doubles then he will expect to win sixty pence multiplied by two, which of course is twenty pence more than the pound you would lose if you refused the double. Mathematically speaking what he is expecting to win is known as the *plus expectation* while your loss is known as the *minus expectation*.

Let's make these terms clearer with an example: you have two men remaining, one each on your 2- and 4-points, while your opponent has his last two men on his 1- and 2-points. It is your turn to roll. Obviously your opponent is in a position to finish the game in one roll should he have the chance to make that roll. But what about you? If you refer to the bearing off table in Chapter I, you will see that you have 23 out of 36 ways to end the game and win one original unit, leaving 13 out of 36 ways in which you will lose the game and thus lose one unit. So if we assume that you arrive in this position 36 times, then you will expect to win 23 times and to lose 13 times. Don't forget that even though the laws of probability are not the laws of prophecy, there is an amazing regularity even for random events that makes the outcome of success or failure very close to the theoretical value of probability. So, we are expecting to win 23 of the games and lose the other 13, therefore we are expecting to win $23-13=10$ games net, or $\frac{10}{36}$ of the original unit, which represents your *plus expectation* since $\frac{10}{36}$ is in this instance positive. Now if you double you will of course expect your plus expectation to double as well – provided that the double is accepted – in which case your plus expectation now becomes $2\times\frac{10}{36}=\frac{20}{36}$ of the original unit. The fact that you *have* a plus expectation ($\frac{10}{36}$ of the original unit), gives you the right to double in this case.

Now let's look at the position from your opponent's angle. If he refuses the double he automatically loses one unit, but if he accepts, then your plus expectation of $\frac{20}{36}$ of the original unit is his *minus expectation*. Therefore the difference for him between refusing the double and losing one unit, and accepting the double with a minus expectation of $\frac{20}{36}$ is $\left[(-1)-(-\frac{20}{36})\right]=-\frac{16}{36}$, which justifies acceptance of the double offered.

Mathematically speaking, there are two basic factors which must be considered when deciding to offer a double:
i) the number of pips (or rolls) left for each player; ii) the positions of both players.

There are similarly two basic factors to be considered when deciding to accept a double:
i) the possibility of losing a double game (gammon); ii) whether the odds in favour of your

opponent are more or less than 3 to 1.

Now to the big question – when should you double? We've seen that the cube may be used at any stage of the game by either player, but there are tremendous differences between using it in a tournament, or when playing for money, or in a chouette. We shall therefore look at each of these situations separately.

SECTION B. THE USE OF THE CUBE IN TOURNAMENT PLAY

Firstly, let's look at an example which I saw occur during a weekly junior tournament at the Clermont Club. It was a seven-point match and the players had reached the position in Diagram 234. The cube was at 4 on Black's side and the score was 4–2 to Red. It was Black to roll: he threw 6–5 and lost the game and match.

I asked Black afterwards why he hadn't doubled. It took him a few minutes to understand the question! Let's analyse why Black had to double at this juncture: the cube was on 4, and Black, to win this game though not the match, had to roll 6–6 or 5–5 – so it was 17 to 1 against him winning. Red on the other hand, if Black didn't roll a winning 6–6 or 5–5, would have won both

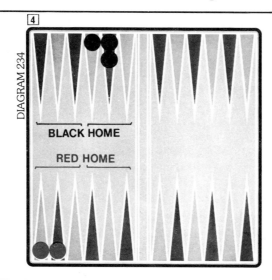

DIAGRAM 234

BLACK HOME

RED HOME

game and match, by 8–2. Even if Black did win this game he would still only lead by 6–4 so Red would have at least one more game to play and could yet save the match. But if Black had doubled to 8, although not increasing his chances of winning (he would still need double 5 or 6) Red's acceptance of the double would have created an entirely new situation. For then, should Black roll his winning 6–6 or 5–5, he would win the game and the match. In a seven-point match what is the difference between losing 8–2 (the score when Black had not doubled) or 12–2 (had he doubled)? Had the cube been on 8 (and Red would naturally accept the double as it is 17 to 1 against Black rolling double 6 or 5) and with Black about to roll, Red would quite likely have had 'the jitters' for a few seconds until the dice came to rest. However, had this been a money game – well no one can stop you losing your money if you want to! But you can immediately see the recklessness of offering such a double if you had been playing for money.

So in tournaments, remember to handle the cube in a logical way (we shall look at the use of the cube in money games in the next section), and what is even more important, remember that it is sometimes better to 'play the score' rather than the game itself. To clarify this point, let's look at Table 9, which illustrates the 'flow chart' of all the scoring possibilities that may arise between two players in a seven-point match. It shows you, whatever the score may be, the type of game (i.e. single, double, triple) you or your opponent needs to win when the cube is on 1, 2, 4, or 8. A close study of this table is vital in order to know when to double or when to refuse: sometimes giving your opponent a point will not necessarily increase his chances of winning.

In Table 9, line 12, Black is leading 5–1: so if the cube is on 1, Black needs a double game to win the match, whereas if the cube was on 2 he would need only a single game. Now assume that Black is leading 5–2 (line 11) or 5–3 (line 10): as far as winning the match is concerned, Black's position hasn't changed, but for Red it is a different story. Black's lead of 5–1 or 5–2 makes no difference to him, for if the cube is on 2 Red needs a triple game to win the match; if the cube is on 4 he needs a double game; while if it is on 8 he needs only a single game. But if the score is 5–3 to Black then Red needs a double game with the cube on 2 and only a single game with the cube on 4. Obviously it is more difficult to win a double game than a single, and even harder to win a triple game than a double. So remember, when the cube is changing sides not only is the person controlling it important, but also the type of game your opponent needs to win the match.

Now let's suppose that Black, when leading 5–1, was doubled by Red. Mathematically speaking, Black is in the same position if he leads 5–1 or 5–2, so if his game is rather weak here, it would be more sensible for him to give Red a point and start afresh with a better chance of winning the next game. Why? Well, say Black accepts the double and then loses a single game, the score then becomes 5–3; and as we saw from line 10, this has now changed the situation for Red – it is much easier for him to go for the match on the next game. So Black, in giving Red a point from 5–1 to 5–2, is not increasing Red's chances of winning. What Black has to remember here when deciding whether or not to take the double is what may happen to him should things go wrong. At all costs he must avoid losing a triple game, and while he doesn't particularly want to lose a double game at least it would still give him another chance. So study Table 9 carefully: it will give you much useful information about playing in tournaments. (You can evolve similar tables for eleven, thirteen, and seventeen-point matches etc.)

Now we shall look at some examples of how experts use the cube in tournaments.

The use of the cube at the beginning of a tournament game
It would be very good practice for you to carry on playing each of the games shown in these examples for a few throws to judge for yourself if the players were right to offer, accept, or refuse the double in each case, and to see if you can work out the reasoning behind their decisions.

In Diagram 235 Red has doubled to 2. He has 15/36 chances of hitting at least once (with 6–4 he hits twice) and if he is not then hit himself, only 5–5 will prevent him from making his 4-point, or 5–3 – although he could break the bar-point to cover the blot but would probably prefer not to. So it was an 'unpleasant take' for Black and he decided to drop which was a good decision. (Particularly bearing in mind that he was leading in this very important competition, which had a first prize of £5,000!) Red therefore won a single game – one point.

In Diagram 236 Red doubled to 2. Black is too fast, and even if Red does not hit (and he has 9/36 chances with 6–2, 6–1, 5–3, 4–3, and 4–4) he may well make his bar-point thus blocking Black – so Black correctly refused the double. You can see in this example an interesting situation in which a double is offered when both players still have two men at the back!

In Diagram 237 Black doubled to 2. Red was leading 21–20 in a twenty-three-point match. He is on the bar, Black has 12/36 chances of hitting him again and 13/36 chances to make his own 1-point, thus keeping the pressure on Red. This could cause Red to lose a double game, giving Black not just the game but the match as well. So Red correctly conceded, preferring to start a fresh game with a better chance; consequently the score levelled to 21-all. So remember, when a double game may be involved, the loss of which will give your opponent the match – drop!

TABLE 9: FLOW CHART FOR SEVEN-POINTS MATCH (Crawford Rule applies)

S single game   D double game   T triple game

PLAYER A   PLAYER B

	Cube on 8			Cube on 4			Cube on 2			Cube on 1			A	B	Cube on 1			Cube on 2			Cube on 4			Cube on 8		
	T	D	S	T	D	S	T	D	S	T	D	S	↓ SCORE ↓		S	D	T	S	D	T	S	D	T	S	D	T
	24	16	8	12	8	4	6	4	2	3	2	1	← POINTS →		1	2	3	2	4	6	4	8	12	8	16	24
1												●	6	6	●											
2												●	6	5		●		●								
3												●	6	4			●		●		●					
4												●	6	3					●		●					
5												●	6	2						●		●		●		
6												●	6	1						●		●		●		
7												●	6	0								●		●		
8										●		●	5	5		●		●								
9										●		●	5	4			●		●		●					
10										●		●	5	3					●		●					
11										●		●	5	2						●		●		●		
12										●		●	5	1						●		●		●		
13										●		●	5	0								●		●		
14						●		●		●			4	4			●		●		●					
15						●		●		●			4	3					●		●					
16						●		●		●			4	2						●		●		●		
17						●		●		●			4	1						●		●		●		
18						●		●		●			4	0								●		●		
19						●		●					3	3					●		●					
20						●		●					3	2						●		●		●		
21						●		●					3	1						●		●		●		
22						●		●					3	0								●		●		
23			●		●		●						2	2						●		●		●		
24			●		●		●						2	1						●		●		●		
25			●		●		●						2	0								●		●		
26			●		●		●						1	1						●		●		●		
27			●		●		●						1	0								●		●		
28			●		●								0	0								●		●		

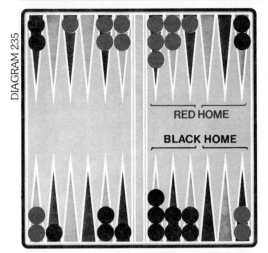

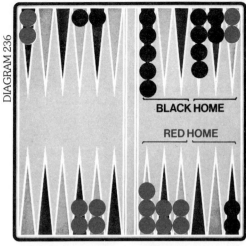

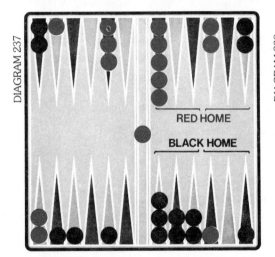

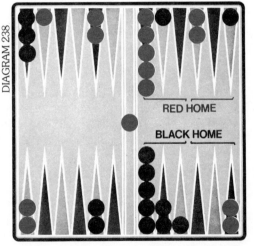

Now look at Diagram 238, Here Black offered a double to 2, and the score was 1–1 in an eleven-point match. Red is on the bar and Black has 14/36 chances of another hit, and another 19/36 chances of making his 4-point. Also he may yet make another point in his home, or his bar-point, thus maintaining pressure on Red, who could then lose a double game and be forced to give Black four points. Much better therefore to drop and give Black just one point.

So far we have seen instances where the double was refused at the beginning of the game due to the fact that the player offering the double had a superior position and thus full control. As a result it was a good idea for the second player to drop. Now let's look at a somewhat different situation. In Diagram 239 Red doubles to 2. The immediate question is, why? Black has opened with 5–2, and Red has not moved at all – yet is offering a double. Well, this game was being played on the second day of a duplicate tournament where 80 games had to be played (40 on each table) and Red and his partner were at this stage way behind. So to try to close the gap they attempted to force each game to be played for 2 points at least (that is for a single game of course). There was no reason for Black to refuse such a double, so he accepted. Red was perfectly correct to double here, so remember when you are very far behind there is justification for doubling in this manner.

If you want to play this game for curiosity's sake, Red's next roll was 2–2 which he played by making his 4- and 11-points, and in the end he managed to win a single game.

In Diagram 240 Red doubled to 2 and he was leading 11–5 in a twenty-three-point match. What one must immediately notice here is that Red is holding Black's 5-point, so if he is hit he at least has some security – something which cannot be said for Black. Now Red, with 6–5, 5–4, 5–3, 5–1, 4–3, 4–1, 3–1, 1–1, and 4–4 can hit and make a point at the same time (16/36 chances); with 5–2, 4–2, and 3–2 he can hit twice (6/36 chances); with 3–3 and 5–5 he can hit twice *and* make a point (2/36 chances), while with 6–4 and 6–6 he can hit only once (3/36 chances). So Red has 29/36 chances of keeping control of the game by putting Black on the bar. With the remaining rolls of 6–3, 6–2, 6–1, 2–1, and 2–2 (9/36 chances) Red will probably make his 5-point to produce a four-point blockade which will be quite difficult for at least one of Black's men to overcome. It would therefore be most unwise for Black to take such a double – but he did. The shock came at the end for him when he lost a triple game, and Red went into the lead by 17–5! Well, it's difficult to 'see' a triple game at this stage but one can predict that it's likely to be at least a single, if not a double, game for Red. *So be careful of accepting a double if you have no anchor in your opponent's homeboard.*

Next look at Diagram 241. Here Red doubled to 2 and he was leading 6–0 in a twenty-three-point match, He is in a very good attacking position with 23/36 chances of hitting once (with 6–5, 6–3, 6–1, 5–4, 5–2, 5–1, 4–3, 4–1, 3–2, 3–1, 2–1, and 1–1) and 10/36 chances of hitting twice (with 6–4, 6–2, 4–2, 2–2, 3–3, 4–4, and 6–6), giving a total of 33/36 chances of at least one hit – and yet the double was accepted. Why? After all Black will more than likely have to play a back game. But notice that he has the most important point in Red's homeboard – the 1-point – and if he is hit can develop a very strong back game; also, his timing is perfect. The end result? Red was not able to accept Black's redouble to 4 in the closing stages of the game! *So beware of doubling a good back game position because you then lose control of the cube.* On the other hand, if you are thinking of accepting such a double, make sure first that you have the basic necessities of holding your opponent's 1-point, and perfect timing.

In Diagram 242 Black has doubled to 2, which is a very interesting proposition: Black is on the bar and he is offering a double. But if you check the two positions you can see immediately that Red is very weak, with three men piled on Black's 1-point (it would be unpleasant for Black

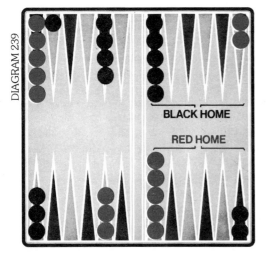

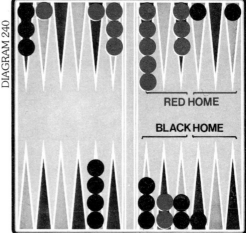

to roll 6–6 now but that's 35 to 1 against). It's a difficult take for Red but it *is* a take (Red is secured in Black's home). So you can imagine Black's feelings when he rolled the dreaded 6–6 followed by Red rolling double 1 – the chances of that happening were 1296 to 1 against. Still, it was a good double by Black in a very interesting situation.

In Diagram 243 Black has doubled to 2, and the score at this stage was 21-all in a twenty-three-point match, with the Crawford Rule in force. Before analysing this particularly interesting situation, I should tell you a little about the two players involved. Both of them were experts, but Red had the most experience with regard to the strategy of the game and handling of the cube. Black stood a good chance of winning a double game and the match and yet he doubled. Why? Well, from Black's viewpoint, if Red drops now then the score will be 22–21 to Black, and in the next game Red will not be able to offer a double (Crawford Rule). So Black would then most probably develop a straightforward running game strategy to win a single game and the match, and even if Red won a single game making the score 22-all, then the cube still cannot be used during the next game. So by doubling now Black is trying to make the cube a 'dead' weapon. Red – quite aware of all this – thought a long time and finally decided to accept the double, so the game then became the deciding one for the match. Once again, you can see here that Red had the security of Black's 1-point, and being on the bar could help him with his timing. This is a beautiful example of how to take advantage of the Crawford Rule. In Section E of this chapter we shall deal in more detail with the importance of knowing your opponent.

The use of the cube in the middle of a tournament game

In Diagram 244 Red doubled to 2. This may look a very 'cheeky' double, but in fact it displays a great understanding of the use of the cube. Both players have three men at the back, but Red cannot be blocked as all his men are on Black's 4-point. The fact that they are all on the same point means that he can use one of them to come out and hit without breaking his anchor. Also it is his roll and he can either hit or block. So Black, taking into consideration that he had a good lead, not surprisingly decided to drop instead of becoming involved in a game controlled by his opponent.

Now look at Diagram 245; Red has doubled to 2, a good example of a player doubling because he is *behind* in the scoring. The pip counts are 137 for Black and 141 for Red, and Black here demonstrates his good 'point management' by giving Red a point and dropping. It is not that the double is untakeable, but it is better not to do so here.

DIAGRAM 241

RED HOME

BLACK HOME

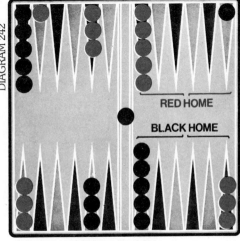

DIAGRAM 242

RED HOME

BLACK HOME

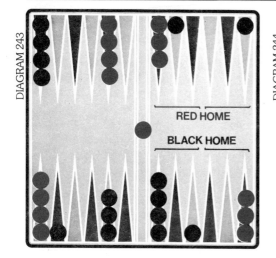

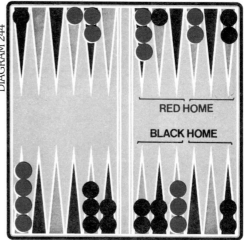

In the example in Diagram 246, Black doubled to 2 in a twenty-three-point match, when the score was 6–4 to Black. Red is on the bar and Black has 19/36 chances of covering the blot on his 4-point (6–4, 6–1, 5–4, 5–2, 4–3, 4–2, 4–1, 3–1, 1–1, 2–2, or 4–4) and a further 4/36 chances of making his 2-point (6–2, 3–3, or 6–6); so as Black is controlling the game, it would be most unwise for Red to accept such a double.

In Diagram 247 Black doubled to 2, again in a twenty-three-point match, where Red was leading by 12–9. Red already has one man on the bar and Black, with 4–3, 4–2, 3–2, 1–1, 2–2, 3–3, and 4–4 (10/36 chances) can hit again and cover at the same time; with 6–4, 6–3, 6–2, 6–1, 5–4, 5–3, 5–2, 4–1, 3–1, and 2–1 he can hit again without covering (20/36 chances), and with 5–5 and 6–6 he can make two more points simultaneously. He very definitely has control of the game, while Red cannot even develop a proper back game, is in a very weak position, and so should not take the double.

In Diagram 248 Black doubled to 2. Black (with 4–3, 1–1, 3–3, and 5–5) can hit again putting a second Red man on the bar while pointing at the same time (5/36 chances); with 6–5, 6–4, 6–3, 5–4, 5–3, 4–2, 4–1, 3–2, 3–1, and 2–1 (20/36 chances) he can hit again without making a point. Red on the other hand cannot develop any proper strategy at all, has no control over the game, or any way of achieving it later, so he must drop.

So far in this section we have looked at examples where one player doubled in the middle of the game and his opponent conceded. Now we shall look at some instances where the double was accepted and analyse the reasons. First in Diagram 249, Black has doubled to 2. He has the better position but he still has a great deal of work to do. He has 17/36 chances of making an extra point in his homeboard, hitting at the same time. Red on the other hand has a good position in Black's homeboard with an anchor, and he is aware that at this stage Black is short of builders with which to enlarge his blockade. Therefore the double is a take for Red.

In Diagram 250 Black has doubled to 2. He has no chance of winning a double game (his pip count is 92 to Red's 141) and with 6–6 will be forced to leave a blot. Even if he doesn't roll a double 6 he still has five men to bring in, so Red must take this double: he has a good board and a long shot for Black will now weaken his position – in fact his next roll was 6–5.

In Diagram 251 Red has doubled to 2, and again we have an instance where a player who is behind in the race, and with only five more games to go, is offering a double to try to increase the point-stake. Fair enough. But Black is not in an inferior position: he is quite strong at the back and at the same time is partially blocking Red's back men. Thus he has good control of the

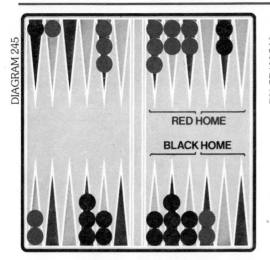

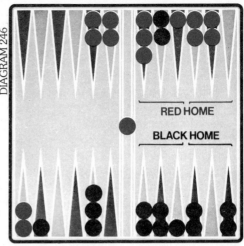

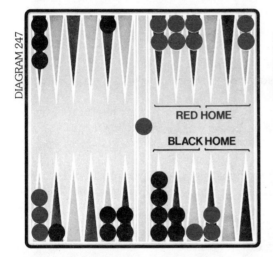

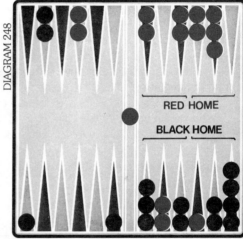

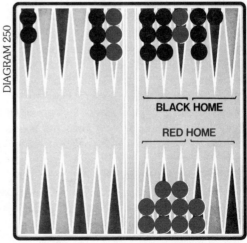

board and all in all it's a take. (Red's next roll was 6–2.)

In Diagram 252 Red doubled to 2, when Black was leading 3–1 in an eleven-point match. This is a very interesting double, since both players are on the bar. Red has 22/36 chances of entering and hitting again to leave Black with two men on the bar, 10/36 chances of entering and playing, and only 6–4, 4–4, and 6–6 (4/36 chances) preventing him from playing at all. So it's a very good double but it *is* a take – because Red has four men at the back while Black may have three at the most. Black also has a partial blockade: so it was the perfect time to offer a double. (Red's next roll was 3–2.)

In Diagram 253 Red has doubled to 2. Black's count is 86, Red's is 89, and it is the latter's roll. The good throws for him are 6–5, 5–4, 5–1, 4–3, 4–1, 3–2, 3–1, 2–1, 1–1, 5–5, and 6–6, giving a total of 19/36 chances of avoiding leaving a blot. With 6–4, 6–2, 5–3, 4–2, 2–2, 3–3, and 4–4 he will be forced to give a shot exposed to a 10 (11/36 chances), while with 6–3 and 5–2 (4/36 chances) he will leave a blot exposed to a 9, and with 6–1 he leaves two blots exposed to 10 and 2. Black on the other hand still has a man on his 8-point available to play 6 (excluding double 6 which is of course the best throw he could hope for) without him having to break his anchor in Red's home: so – it's a take.

Next see Diagram 254. Here Black has doubled to 2 and it was a double he had to offer. He is blocking four of Red's men while Red is only blocking two of Black's, and Black has a good chance of producing a five-point blockade. Red though, while he would obviously prefer not to be doubled, is blocking from a distance, making it more difficult for Black to come out; whereas Red himself can overcome Black's blockade with a direct shot, a 6. (The nearer you are to a blockade the more chance you have of getting out – direct shots versus long shots.) Hence the double is acceptable.

Finally, in Diagram 255 Black has doubled to 2. Red is on the bar, already has five men at the back, and can be hit again (with 6–1 or 4–3) – but the fact that he is holding Black's 1- and 5-points justifies his take of the double. Black does not yet have a proper block and Red's timing is good.

Now we have seen the use of the doubling cube at the beginning and in the middle of the game, sometimes being accepted and sometimes not. Lastly we shall see the cube in use at the end of the game.

The use of the cube at the end of a tournament game

Here we shall look at two different situations: firstly, where neither player has started to bear off, and secondly, where one or both players are in the bearing off process.

In Diagram 256 Black has doubled to 4. Red was leading 6–0 in a twenty-three-point match, but you can see from the diagram that he has a problem with his two back men – whereas Black has a very good board and enough spare men to wait for Red to come to him for punishment! Not surprisingly Red conceded.

In Diagram 257 Black doubled to 4; it was a twenty-three-point match and Red was leading 20–19. The score here speaks for itself: with the cube on 4 it is enough for Black to win a single game to take the match as well. This, plus the fact that Red is on the bar and Black has the opportunity for another hit, makes it an untakeable double.

In the next example, Black has doubled to 4 (Diagram 258). As you can see Black has by now lost any chance of winning a double game. Red's count is 66 and Black's 52 (and it's him to roll of course); so why give Red the chance of rolling double 6 or 5 which would then enable him to take advantage of his faster board? Also if Black rolls 6–3 he will have to leave a blot, so he must offer a double, but because it's Black to roll Red cannot take it.

In Diagram 259 Red has doubled to 4! Black has 11/36 chances of entering, but with 2–4, 2–2, and even 2–3 (Red would probably move a man off Black's 5-point to enable Black to move

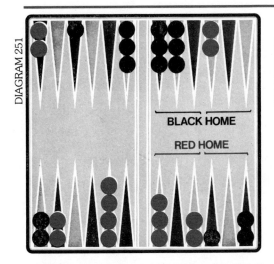

DIAGRAM 251

BLACK HOME

RED HOME

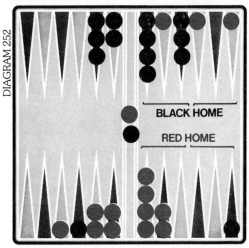

DIAGRAM 252

BLACK HOME

RED HOME

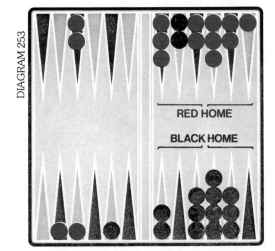

DIAGRAM 253

RED HOME

BLACK HOME

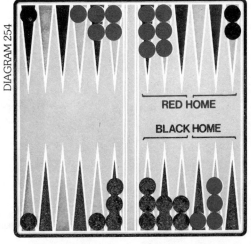

DIAGRAM 254

RED HOME

BLACK HOME

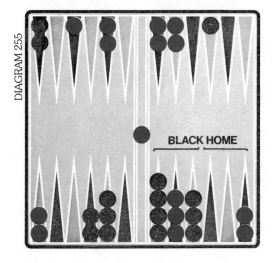

DIAGRAM 255

BLACK HOME

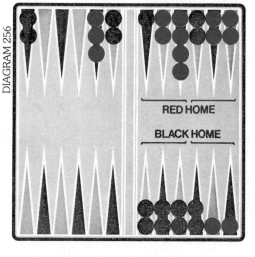

DIAGRAM 256

RED HOME

BLACK HOME

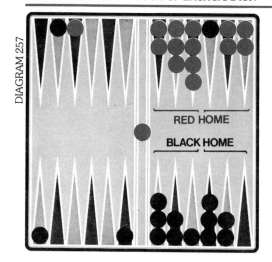

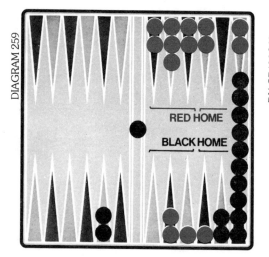

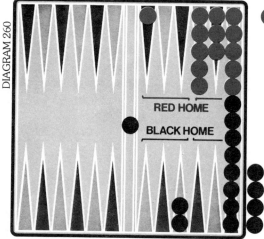

a 3) Black will be forced to leave two more blots. Therefore Black is not favoured to win and he correctly dropped.

Now some examples where one or both players are in the process of bearing off. First Diagram 260, where Red has doubled to 4. There is no roll that can force Red to leave a blot, while Black needs at least three rolls to bring his man back home and carry on bearing off (only double 6, double 5, and – though not so good a roll – double 4, will ease his position). By this time Red will have taken more of his men off, thereby cancelling Black's advantage – and Red is one roll ahead with his turn now, so Black (correctly) conceded.

In Diagram 261 Red has doubled to 4. It is an interesting situation and we should analyse it carefully. Red can hit once with 6–4, 6–3, 6–2, 5–4, 5–3, 5–2, 4–1, 3–2, 2–2, and 4–4 (18/36 chances) and twice with 4–3, 4–2, 3–1, 2–1, and 3–3 (9/36 chances) giving a total of 27/36 chances of his hitting at least once: in other words he is 3 to 1 *on*. Should Black take the double when Red has odds in his favour of exactly 3 to 1? Well, let's see what may happen if Red rolls 6–5, 6–1, 5–1, 1–1, 5–5, and 6–6 (9/36 chances): he cannot hit, but Black with 6–3, 5–3, 4–3, 4–1, 3–3, and 4–4 will still be forced to leave a blot (10/36 chances) and with 3–3 he has

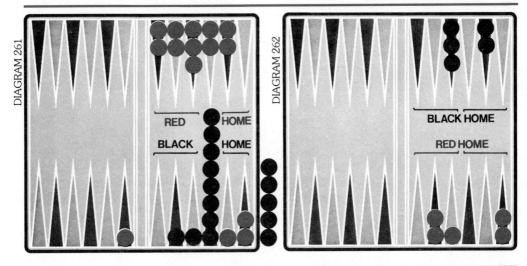

to leave two blots. If Black were in such a position that nothing would force him to leave a blot, so that he could be sure of not being hit, then he could be brave and take this double – but when Red has the opportunity of hitting again even after missing the first time, Black has no option but to refuse.

In Diagram 262 Red has doubled to 8. Here we have a 'five men versus five men' situation. Black does have a slight advantage should he roll a double, but if he rolls a regular roll then Red will have the advantage – and don't forget it's Red to roll first. He has 20/36 chances of bearing off one man and 14/36 chances of bearing off two men, whereas Black, who rolls second, will have 19/36 chances of bearing off one man leaving 13/36 chances to bear off two men. So Black was right to concede.

Study these examples again and again; they will give you a good idea of how and when – and *why* – to use the doubling cube to your advantage.

Lastly, a word about the opening moves when playing in a tournament. It is important in this situation to *play to the score* and therefore to be able to adapt your opening moves to your position at the time. For instance, if you need only one point to win the match, then it's quite sensible if you have an opening roll of 6–2 to run with one of your back men in order to try to develop a straightforward running strategy. But if you need *two* points, then it would be better to bring a builder all the way to your 5-point, to try to develop a blocking strategy. Or you could move one of your back men the 6, and bring a builder round to your 11-point to play the 2 – to develop a blocking-running strategy. Alternatively, if your opponent needs only one point to win the match and you are way behind, then adopt a block-chance move, because you want to complicate the game as much as possible for him.

SECTION C. THE USE OF THE CUBE WHEN PLAYING FOR MONEY

We saw in the previous section that the decisive factor in the use of the doubling cube was logic or common sense. If that's the case in tournaments, why not in money games too? Well, no one will actually say it isn't, but still there is a tremendous difference between the two. In a tournament, if you take the wrong double it may cost you not only the game, but the match as well – and then you are out and have to wait until next week, next month, or next year to have another go. But if you are playing for money and you take a wrong double, and even (heaven forbid) find yourself losing 32 points in one game – well it may be very painful, but you still have a chance in the next game! And that thought of the 'next game' is the mainstay of irrational players who tend to accept almost any double offered. Quite often you will hear players trying to justify taking a double wrongly with a quite unjustifiable statement – such as 'I am steaming!' (meaning 'I am losing a lot!'). Why the fact that they are losing a lot should suddenly cause 'Lady Luck' to start shining on them and not on their opponent as previously, is something I have never been able to fathom. So try to remember when playing for money not to let the score affect you and force you to take wrong doubles. You must develop self-control over this temptation; for more about the psychological side of playing see Section E of this chapter.

You may ask 'what is the secret when playing for money?' I would answer in one word – run! As simply and as quickly as possible, run, and try to bring the game into your favour. This applies to any stage of the game, but obviously in particular to the beginning of the game. That is why it's good strategy to make use of those opening moves that start your men running (see Chapter II). What is even more important, you must be aware – and be able to take advantage – of any opportunity in the middle of the game that will enable you to bring the game to its crucial moment. To illustrate this point, we shall look at an outstanding example.

In Diagram 263 Black has to play 6–4. If you study the diagram carefully you will see that there is only one play which will enable Black to win (and quite possibly even win a gammon), and that is as shown in Diagram 264. Black has hit with the 4 and come out with one of his back men – thus bringing the game to its climax. Black needed two points to win this set otherwise he would find himself right out of the picture, for Red was leading one set to love in a three-set series (each set consisting of a five-point match). Now let's analyse the risk Black is taking with this move. Red, with 6–5, 6–3, 6–1, 5–1, 3–1, 1–1, 3–3, 5–5, and 6–6 (14/36 chances) cannot enter; with 5–2 or 3–2 he can come in on the 2, but will have a problem with the 5 or the 3 (4/36 chances); with 2–1 he comes in on the 2 and will probably use the 1 to make his 1-point (2/36 chances). This gives a total of 20/36 chances that Black will keep the timing. With 4–2 or 4–3 Red can enter and hit with the 4, but will again have a problem with the 2 or 3 (he has two blots in his homeboard) thus giving Black 24/36 chances of maintaining control; while with 6–4, 6–2, 5–4, or 2–2 Red can enter and hit, but will still have to leave at least one blot in his home giving Black 7/36 chances to remain in the game. The only really bad shots for Black would be 4–1 or 4–4 (3/36 chances) when Red would hit with the 4 and with the 1, cover his 1-point, or with the remaining three 4s would probably hit again, twice. So Black, by moving as shown in Diagram 264, took a good 'controlled' risk.

Now, as for tournaments, we shall look at the use of the cube at the beginning, in the middle, and at the end of money games.

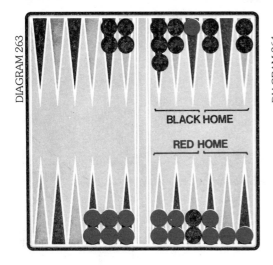

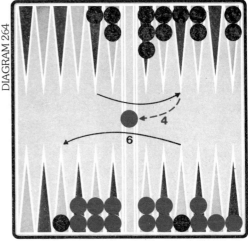

BLACK HOME

RED HOME

The use of the cube at the beginning of a money game

First look at Diagram 265, Here Black is doubling to 2; Red is behind in a weak position with Black blocking him. Black is also holding his opponent's bar-point and Red has no real chance of gaining control of the game – so quite correctly he dropped. *(Note the combination of Black's blockade plus the security of holding Red's bar-point.)*

In Diagram 266 Red has doubled to 2 in a five-point match (being played for money) where Black was leading 3–0. Black is on the bar and Red with 6–5, 6–4, 6–3, 6–2, 5–4, 5–3, 5–2, 5–1, 4–3, 4–1, 3–2, 3–1, 2–1, 1–1, 2–2, 3–3, 4–4, and 6–6 can hit again (20/36 chances); then Black, with two men on the bar, will be 3 to 1 against bringing both men in with one roll. Rightly he conceded.

The use of the cube in the middle of a money game

In Diagram 267 Red has doubled to 4. It was an obvious double: Red had a good blockade against Black's two back men, and with 6–2, 5–3, 5–2, 4–2, 3–2, 2–1, and 2–2 he could have hit again (13/36 chances). In that case Black might well have lost a double game, which would mean 8 points. So he dropped.

In Diagram 268 Red doubled to 2 – and it's a very cheeky double! There are 4/36 chances that he won't be able to play (6–5, 6–6, and 5–5) but he has 23/36 chances of hitting once (6–4, 6–3, 6–2, 6–1, 5–3, 5–2, 5–1, 4–2, 3–2, 3–1, 2–1, and 1–1), and 9/36 chances of hitting *twice* (5–4, 4–3, 4–1, 2–2, 3–3 and 4–4). So in total he has 32/36 chances of keeping his good position. One would have to be very brave to take such a double.

In Diagram 269 Red doubled to 2, He has a five-point blockade, which as far as Black is concerned (with his man on the 1-point) might just as well be a prime – because he needs the miracle roll of 6–1 against which the odds are 17 to 1. Even then Red will have 26/36 chances of hitting back (any 5 or 3). It's true that Black is blocking two Red men with a five-point blockade, but he will have to start breaking it very soon; also Red has three spare men to play so can thus keep his good position, *and* he has an anchor in Black's homeboard. This is an example of a 'steamy' double – and it was not surprising that Black lost a single game needlessly costing him two points instead of one.

Now look at Diagram 270, Here Black has doubled to 2, and both players have three men at the back. But Red's are better placed, and he is slightly ahead; only a 5 will enable Black to hit and even then Red won't be out of the game, He has more control of the outerboards should

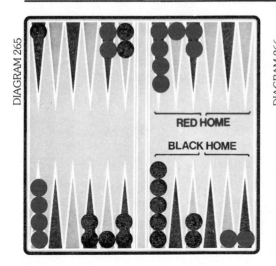

DIAGRAM 265

RED HOME

BLACK HOME

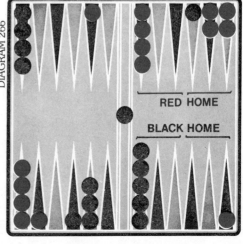

DIAGRAM 266

RED HOME

BLACK HOME

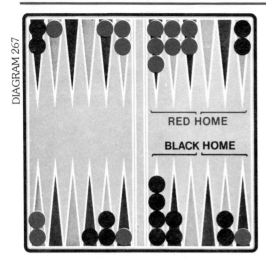

DIAGRAM 267

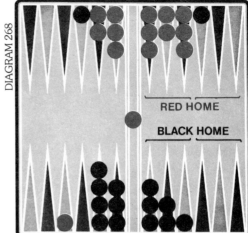

DIAGRAM 268

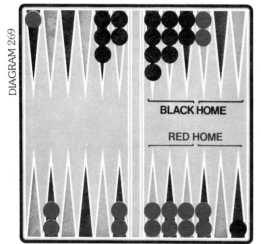

DIAGRAM 269

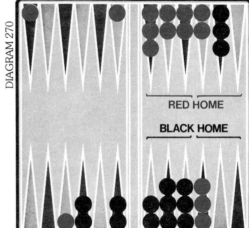

DIAGRAM 270

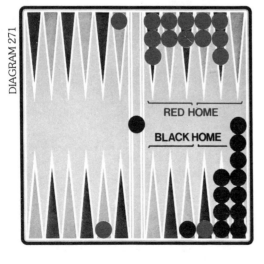

DIAGRAM 271

Black have to come out without hitting. So it's a take, but in a way this was a double offered too early for both players still have much to do. And towards the end of the game Black couldn't take the redouble.

The use of the cube at the end of a money game

There is not much difference at this stage between the use of the cube in tournaments and its use in money games (see Section B, The use of the cube at the end of a tournament game). Here is just one more example, the situation mentioned above in Diagram 270 when Black was offered a redouble. See Diagram 271. Red has doubled to 4. Black is on the bar and his good rolls are 3–1, 2–1, and 1–1 which will enable him to come in and save the blot in his homeboard. With 5–1 or 4–1 he can enter but cannot save the second blot, while with 6–1 he comes in, goes out – hitting – but still leaves two blots. Thus it is an untakeable double!

SECTION D.   CHOUETTE

Chouette is a form of backgammon where at least three players participate. Each player rolls one die and the person rolling the highest number is then known as 'the man in the box'; whoever rolled the next highest number becomes the 'captain', and the remaining players form his 'team' but succeed to the captaincy according to the numbers they have rolled. In the case of a tie between players, they (and only they) roll again to determine their positions in the team.

Anyone may join the chouette at any stage (provided all the players agree of course) by becoming the last player in the team. The newcomer should obviously join the team at the beginning of a fresh game, i.e. he cannot normally join the team in the middle of a game, unless the players agree to make an exception. The game is played between the man in the box and the captain, the rest of the team being partners to the captain. As far as scoring is concerned, the man in the box is playing separately against each member of the team; so if he wins a single game, he wins a single game from *each* player and remains in the box while the captain loses his place and becomes the last member of the team. The new captain is then the player who was next in line to the old captain. But if the man in the box loses a single game, then he loses a single game to *each* player in the team, comes out of the box, and becomes the last player in the team. The next man in the box is the previous captain, while the player next to him becomes the new captain, and so on.

The captain may consult his partners (the rest of the team) during the game but the final decision on a move is his, and the partners are bound by the captain's word. If the man in the box doubles, each team member decides individually whether to accept or refuse the double. If the captain wishes to refuse it, then he drops out of the game and is replaced by the next member of the team who is willing to accept it. The order of the team members is not affected by the acceptance or refusal of a double. Those players who concede are out of that particular game and cannot be consulted by the captain. If a team member wants to leave one particular game for a time he can either ask one of his partners to act for him, or else remain in the game under the captain's jurisdiction. When a player wishes to leave the *chouette* temporarily, he must say so and his score will then be frozen until he returns – when he joins the end of the team as a new player would. If any individual member of the team (including the captain) wants to double, say from 1 to 2, then he may offer any one member of the team one point; if they accept he takes over their game. This process is called 'giving for game'. But the man in the box has the privilege of pre-empting any or part of this deal and he will then take over their game.

Any kind of settlement can occur in chouette. Sometimes when there are more than five players the box may take a partner from the team – although he cannot choose the captain. The partner then acts in the box in the same way as if he were a member of the team. If the box is doubled the partner may drop, in which case the man in the box then takes over the points paid by his partner and must now play for the double stake. Similarly if the man in the box wants to drop then his partner may take over.

When the box doubles, two players may do a 'drop-take', that is, they agree to drop one game and to take on the other *together*. In this case, both players are still in the game.

So much for the method of play: now we shall look at the strategy.

The strategy in chouette

1. Putting pressure on the man in the box
The man in the box playing against, say, four players will automatically be playing for four points. So if the team double the box early on in the game, and the man in the box accepts it, he will then have to play for at least eight points. If the captain is the better player, it is quite likely that the box will drop.

2. Relieving the pressure
a) If you manage to come to an overwhelmingly strong position, then normally you would go for a double game and not offer a double. However, if you are in the box in this situation you should double because it is more than likely that one or two of the team will drop – and then even if something goes wrong you stand a good chance of at least breaking even.
b) After the box has accepted a double, you (as a member of the team) may offer to take a point (or give a point according to the circumstances). Quite probably the man in the box will be happy to rid himself of some of the pressure being put upon him. This, incidentally, is one of the best ways to collect points in chouette; try to build up a 'bank' of points in order to make your position easier when you enter the box.

3. Giving for game
Don't become a player who always 'gives for game' just to improve his situation. Improvements don't come via hopeless doubles!

4. Being the man in the box – advantage or disadvantage?
Checking some forty chouettes that I have on record (five players in each) shows that on average the box is a loser. True, forty games may not be enough to form any definite conclusions, but it would be a good idea to bear the possibility in mind. If you go into the box knowing that the captain is a much better player than you, it's obviously sensible to drop and lose a point rather than stay in the box and lose more. You will always find someone 'steaming' who will be only too happy to take your box!

SECTION E.   PSYCHOLOGY AND BACKGAMMON

'It is true that only one out of a hundred wins, but what is that to me?'

Fyodor Dostoevsky – *The Gambler*

Backgammon is not played in a vacuum. Individuals are involved – you and your opponent (or opponents) and each player has his own personality and different weaknesses. One person may act rationally and another quite irrationally. So it's a must to know a little about the psychology of playing backgammon if you really want to be able to make the best possible decisions.

Fouraker and Siegel[*] classified players' personalities into three distinct categories:
a) The simple maximizer;   b) the rivalist;   c) the co-operator.

The simple maximizer is primarily interested in his own pay-off, whereas the rivalist is primarily interested in doing better than his partner (or partners), his own pay-off being of secondary interest, while the co-operator will help both himself and his partner. Everybody has

[*]*Bargaining and Group Decision Making by L. E. Fouraker and S. Siegel (McGraw-Hill 1960)*

different attitudes towards risk, and it's difficult – in fact it's impossible – to 'measure' personality. But the research done by Fouraker and Siegel has given us some vital, if basic, information.

When playing for money, a player will make different decisions from those he will make playing for token-money, i.e. chips. He may act rationally and choose from all the available options the course that promises to *maximize* the expected pay-off (e.g. doubling at the right time) or *minimize* the expected loss (e.g. not taking 'steamy' doubles). Alternatively he may act irrationally, like the player with an incomplete grasp of the doubling process. You yourself will obviously react differently towards the irrational player who tends to take any double, and the rational player who is very cautious in his decisions.

You must recognise your opponent's goals and how he is likely to go about reaching them. What motivates him? Is his behaviour the same when playing in front of a few people as when he plays in front of a large crowd? Or does he then make wild decisions just to keep up the excitement? Can he afford to lose and still enjoy the game? Or is he under the pressure of his pocket – something that could lead him to a wrong decision? Does he make wise decisions when playing 'bad' rolls? What is his knowledge of the theory of the game? And above all – is he an expert who knows all the tricks of the game? After all, it's well known that certain strategies count on errors being made by a fallible human opponent! Quite often an expert will offer a double at the 'wrong' time when playing for money against a moderate player, knowing that his opponent will probably drop and therefore give him a point. Should his opponent unexpectedly take the double, he still has the security of his superior skill to turn the game back into his favour.

You must, at all stages of the game, know exactly what you want to do, and in which direction the game needs to be developed – otherwise you will just be shuffling the men around and not really playing. Alice's conversation with the Cat in *Alice in Wonderland* by Lewis Carroll is a most apt parallel:

'"Would you tell me, please, which way I ought to go from here?"

"That depends a good deal on where you want to get to", said the Cat.

"I don't much care", said Alice.

"Then it doesn't matter which way you go", said the Cat.'

Quite!

You must also be aware of what type of strategy you need to adopt before starting to play – and remember what your opponent may do to counteract it. Suppose you need one point to win the match in a tournament, then you might well reason that a running strategy would be best suited to achieve this – so try to think what your opponent will do to defend against it. Be prepared.

Since backgammon is governed by the outcome of the dice, people tend to blame their failure on 'Lady Luck' rather than admit that their opponent was more skilful. But is it always luck? We all know that the game is a combination of skill (the personality) and luck (the dice) and neither component can be measured. But we can learn about the personality of our opponent by acquainting ourselves with his behaviour, his skill, and how he uses it. It is not understanding the outcome of a phenomenon which is frustrating, so that we just whisper 'unlucky' in resigned tones! If someone tosses a coin in the air, then the probability (which is a measure of uncertainty) of a particular outcome being achieved can be calculated from the results of repeated experiments; and the unknown factors that operate to produce these results are attributed to *chance*. So it is 'chance' – a synonym for these unknown factors – that most people are talking about when they mention 'luck'.

Sometimes certain people do appear to be exceptionally lucky, winning all the time. Often this may be based on intuitive judgements – and if you followed their scores over a long period you would probably find that they don't always win. So there's no sense in trying to rate skill and luck in percentages, but what we can say is this: the more skill you possess, the more chance you have of eliminating the role that luck plays – up to a point. Why 'up to a point'? Well, if your opponent rolls a series of double 6s in the last stages of the game, all the skill in the world won't help you: he'll win.

Try not to play with the same people all the time or you will very soon find yourself falling into a set pattern of play and you will not improve your game. And don't underestimate your opponent: many a game has been lost because of such a mistaken attitude. When you are playing for money, always play according to what you can afford to lose rather than what you would like to win – otherwise you can find yourself in some very unpleasant situations. When playing for money with a person you don't know it's a good idea to play for small stakes, at least until you get to know him better. Always keep a cool head: don't show your opponent that you are upset, and never give up. Keep your determination to win, even if you are nine points down in an eleven-point match – you still have a chance if you want to take it. Above all, have confidence in yourself. But if sometimes you find things are persistently going wrong, leave the board alone for a few days: don't try and push your 'luck' because it won't work. Come back to the game when you feel fresh again. And lastly, when playing concentrate only on the game, leave all your problems behind you and 'isolate' yourself in backgammon.

Remember: self-control and skill and will . . . and a little bit of luck . . . will make you win!

APPENDIX

Backgammon for Beginners

HOW THE GAME IS PLAYED

A. Number of players

There are two players in a game of backgammon, whom we shall call Player A and Player B, playing against each other. (There is another version of the game, called chouette, in which more than two players can participate.)

B. Equipment

The Board

The backgammon board, as you can see from Diagrams 272 and 273, is divided into four parts, each of which is known as a *table*. The central partition is called *the bar*. On either side of the bar there are two tables, each containing six triangles known as *points*. Thus there are 24 of these points, marked alternately in two different colours. (The colours have no special significance.)

The board is placed between the players with the bar lying vertically between them, so that six points lie to the right and left of each player. One of the tables – either to the right or left of the bar – is the inner board of Player A (or his *homeboard*) and the table on the other side of the bar is the *outerboard* of Player A. Opposite him, Player B has the same arrangement, so that both Player A's and Player B's homeboards are on the same side of the bar, and the outerboards are on the other side of the bar. (Whether to have the homeboards on the right or left of the bar will be dealt with later.)

The Men (see Diagrams 274 and 275)

There are thirty men altogether, divided so that Player A has fifteen all of one colour, and Player B has the other fifteen, all of a different colour.

The Dice

Each player has a pair of standard dice – each die being numbered from one to six inclusive, with one number on each face.

The Dice Cups

Each player has his own dice cup in which to shake and roll his dice.

The Doubling Die (The Cube)
The doubling die is used to double or redouble the game. It is usually larger than the playing dice; on each face is printed one of the numbers 2, 4, 8, 16, 32, or 64. (The method of doubling is explained in Chapter VIII.)

C. Preparation for play
Any decision about where to sit, which colour men to have, or which side the homeboard should be, is settled either by gentleman's agreement or by using the dice. By that system, each player rolls one die from his dice cup until one of them has rolled a higher number. That player then has the right to make the decisions mentioned above. (The dice must land flat on the board, otherwise they are known as *void* or *cocked* dice and the player concerned must roll again.)

D. Setting up the board at the start of the game
Once it has been established where each player will have his homeboard, which automatically defines where his outerboard will be, the men are placed on the board for the start of the game. (Incidentally, there is no advantage whatsoever to the player who chooses on which side the homeboards will be.) But first let us look at Diagrams 272 and 273, and identify the different parts of the board.

The homeboard: the nearest point to the bar within the homeboard is called point number 6 (or the sixth, or 6-point); while the furthest point from the bar within the homeboard is called point number 1 (or the first, or 1-point).

The outerboard: the nearest point to the bar within the outerboard is the seventh point (or, as it is more commonly called, the bar-point); the furthest point from the bar within the outerboard is identified as the 12th point. The points on the other side of the board (i.e. on your opponent's home and outerboards) are identified in the same way. Therefore each homeboard contains the points 1 to 6 inclusive, and each outerboard contains the points 7 to 12 inclusive. So each player, A and B, has six points (1 to 6) in his homeboard and six points (7 to 12) in his outerboard. As you can see from Diagrams 272 and 273, whether the points run from left to right or vice versa entirely depends on which side the homeboard is. The implications of this identification are: a) the first point of Player A is the 24th point for Player B (and vice versa);   b) The sixth

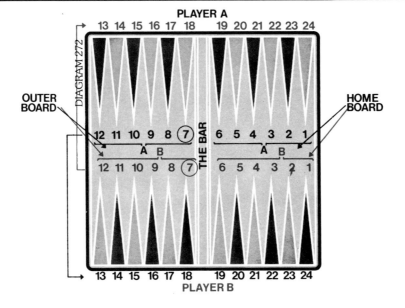

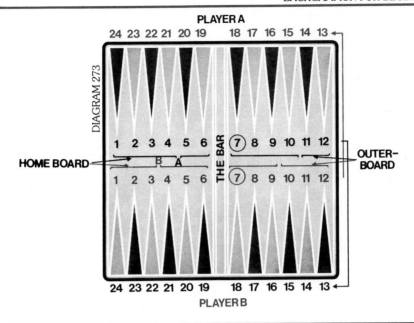

point of Player A is the 13th point for Player B (and vice versa);   c) The 12th point of player A is the 13th point for Player B (and vice versa). All the other points can be identified in the same manner.

We have now identified all the points on the board, and can start to set it up. Each player places five of his men on his sixth point (in his homeboard), three more on his eighth point (in his outerboard), five more on his 13th point (in his opponent's outerboard) and his last two men on his 24th point (in his opponent's homeboard), so the board looks like Diagram 274. Or, if the homeboard is on the other side, then it will look like Diagram 275. At the beginning of the game the two men on the first points (two belonging to each player) are known as the *back men*.

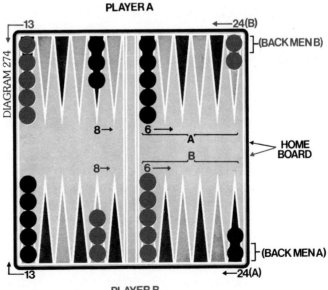

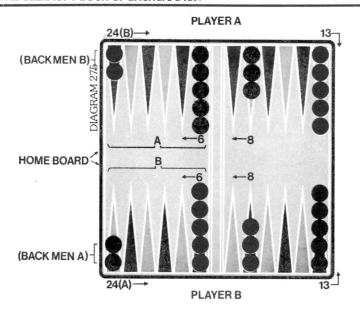

The Direction of Play (see Diagrams 274 and 275)

Each player is allowed to make his moves in the direction indicated, proceeding from his 24-point towards his first point – and he can move *only* in this direction. That means the two players will be moving in opposite directions to each other. Each player starts by moving from his opponent's homeboard along his opponent's outerboard, round to his own outerboard and into his own homeboard.

The Object of the Game

The object of each player is to move his men (in the proper direction of course) round the board into his homeboard and then to take them off the board – this is called *bearing off* the men. You can only begin taking the men off the board when they are *all* in the homeboard – how you do it we shall discuss later.

The end of the game: once a player has managed to bear off all his men the game is over.

Winning the game: the player who has managed to bear off his men first is the winner.

If the loser has managed to bear off at least one man, then the game is called a *single game* and the winner receives one point.

If the loser has not managed to bear off any men but has no men left in his opponent's homeboard or on the bar, then the game is called a *double game* or a *gammon* and is worth two points to the winner, i.e. it is worth two single games.

If the loser fails not only to bear off any men but still has at least one man in his opponent's homeboard or on the bar, then the game is called a *triple game* or a *backgammon* – and the winner receives three points, i.e. the game is worth three single games.

Identification of Types of Point (see Diagram 276)

The 24 points on the board are divided into two different types: firstly, when there are at least two men of the same colour (i.e. belonging to one player) on one point anywhere on the board, then that point is called a *closed point*, or *made* point. Only men of the same colour (i.e. belonging to the same colour) may then land on that point; in fact any or all of that player's men may land on that point at any stage of the game.

If there is only one man, of either colour, on a point – any point – then that point is called an *open point* and the single man on it is a *blot*. If there are no men occupying a certain point, then it is vacant and may also be referred to as an open point. Either player during his move may land with one, or more, men on such a point. If the point was vacant and the player lands with only one man then it is still an open point, but once two men belonging to the same player land on it then it becomes closed. If the open point was already occupied by one man, then a second man belonging to the same player landing on that point makes it closed.

If the open point is occupied by one man belonging to your opponent (i.e. he has a blot on the point) then you may either pass over it or you may (indeed may have to) land on the point. In this instance, since two men of different colours cannot occupy the same point, the blot is said to have been *hit* and is consequently put on the bar (see Diagram 276). It is possible that during the game more than one man (either of the same or different colours) may be on the bar – technically all but one of the men could be on the bar at the same time, although this is highly unlikely!

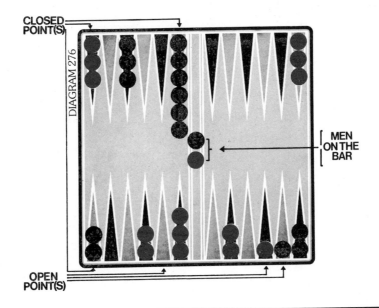

E. Playing the game

The men are moved, once the dice have been rolled and come to rest (if they are cocked they must be rolled again), according to the numbers appearing on the upper faces of the dice. When the numbers on the two dice are different this is known as a *regular roll* (as say, 5–3). Now look at Diagrams 277, 278, 279, and 280.

The complete number on each die is used separately to move one man in the correct direction, while the complete number on the second die may be used to move either the same man again or to move a different man (obviously belonging to the same player). Each number appearing on the upper face of the dice in a regular roll may be used only once in any particular move.

If the dice show the same number on each die, then this is a *doublet* or *double roll* – and each number may be played *twice*. Because the numbers in a doublet are the same this means in effect that the same number is being played *four* times. It doesn't matter if the numbers are used to move one man, two men, three men, or four men, so long as the move is 'legal', i.e. in the right direction and not landing on a closed point held by the opponent. As we said, both numbers

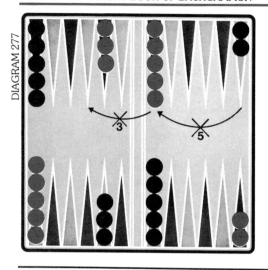

DIAGRAM 277

'ILLEGAL' MOVE OF THE REGULAR ROLL (5–3)

'LEGAL' MOVES OF THE REGULAR ROLL (5–3)

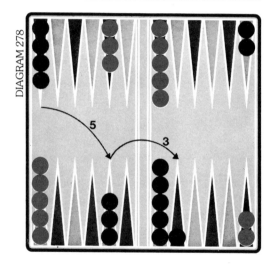

DIAGRAM 278

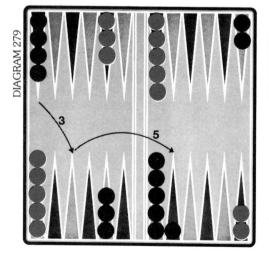

DIAGRAM 279

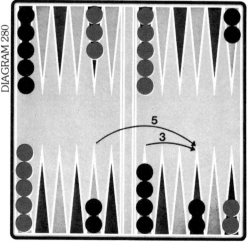

DIAGRAM 280

**PLAYING THE HIGHEST
NUMBER
Black rolled (6–5)**

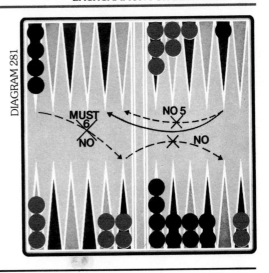

DIAGRAM 281

must be played even if it is inconvenient to the player moving and even if the only move you can make is to hit your opponent's blot or blots.

It is important to remember that with any roll the numbers appearing on the two dice must be played separately and cannot be added together so that you just move the grand total. For example, in Diagram 281, Black has rolled 6–5. If he could add this together and move 11 all at once, then he could use the total roll; but the rules are that the numbers must be treated separately. So looking carefully at the diagram, you can see that Black can use either the 6 or the 5, but not one followed by the other. In cases like this, i.e. when either number can be played but not both, then the higher number *must* be used. If neither number can be played then the player passes his turn and has to wait until his opponent has completed his move before rolling again.

If a player has a man (or men) on the bar then he cannot move until he has brought it (or them) back into the game. This is known as *entering* (or re-entering) from the bar and takes place as follows: when it is his turn, the player with the man or men on the bar rolls the dice, and provided that the number on the upper face of the dice corresponds to either an open point, or a closed point belonging to himself, *in his opponent's homeboard and thus according to his opponent's numbering*, then he may enter a man from the bar on to this point. For instance, if you look at the first example in Diagram 282, Black has rolled 6–5. But Red is holding his own 6-point and his own 5-point (i.e. in his homeboard) so Black cannot enter at all. In the second example, Diagram 283, the 5-point is open, so he can enter on that and then play the 6 elsewhere on the board. He can of course move the same man, out of Red's homeboard, if he so wishes, provided he doesn't land on a closed point held by Red. If both points are open but he cannot move the number of the second die then he must enter on the highest number (i.e. 6) – see Diagram 284. If both points are open and there is no problem about playing the remaining number then he may choose on which point to enter. See Diagram 285.

Failure to enter from the bar disqualifies the player from moving any of his other men: he must enter any man (or all men) from the bar *before* making any other play. Once he has entered it (or them) from the bar he may continue play as normal, so if he had only one man to bring in, he could then use the number on the second die to make a move. If he has two men on the bar then he will have to use both dice to bring in the two men; unless he rolls a double and then if the corresponding point is open and he can enter, the remaining two numbers can be used to move.

DIAGRAM 282

6 5

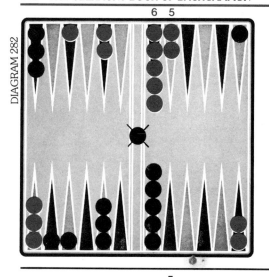

Black has a man on the bar and rolled (6–5), so he cannot play

DIAGRAM 283

5

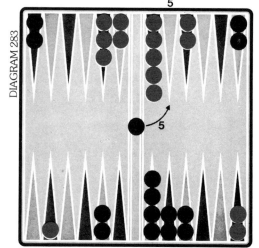

Here Black is forced to enter with the 5, and play the 6 elsewhere on the board

DIAGRAM 284

6 5

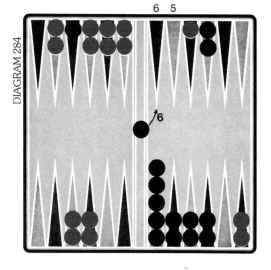

Black can only use one of his numbers – so he must enter with the 6, i.e. use the highest number

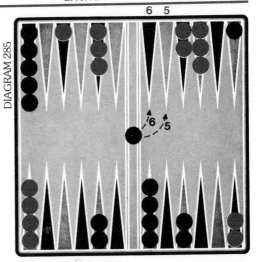

Here Black can use the 6
or the 5 to enter from
the bar

DIAGRAM 285

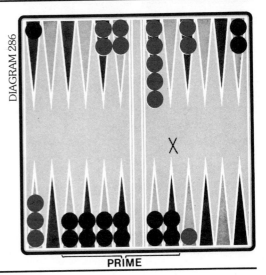

THE PRIME
Red's back man
cannot move

DIAGRAM 286

PRIME

If all the points in his opponent's homeboard are closed, then naturally the player can't enter at all. He must wait until at least one point becomes an open point, though if his opponent leaves a blot then he may enter – if he rolls the right number – and hit it. Incidentally, when a player holds all the points in his own homeboard (i.e. they are all closed), he is said to have a *closed board*. See Diagram 287. So remember, if a player has a man or men on the bar he cannot move until all of them have been brought back into play.

If a player has managed to secure six successive closed points anywhere on the board, it is known as a *prime* – see Diagram 286. The object of a prime is to block the opponent, who will obviously not be able to pass it since *any* number on either die will force him to land on a closed point not belonging to him – and this he cannot do.

Bearing Off

So far we have seen the dice used in two different ways: firstly to move the men round the board and secondly to enter a man from the bar. There is now a third use as the game approaches its final stages. Once a player has managed to bring all his men into his homeboard then he may

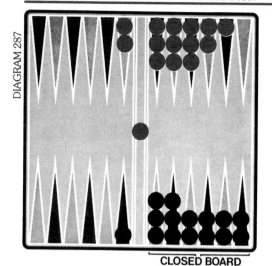

DIAGRAM 287

CLOSED BOARD
Red has a man on the
bar and cannot play

CLOSED BOARD

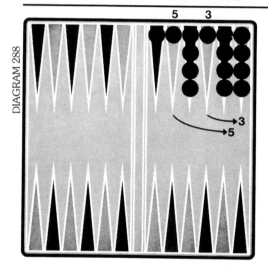

DIAGRAM 288

5   3

BEARING OFF
Black rolled (5–3); he
can bear off two men if
he plays like this

start taking them off the board; but he can only start this process, known as bearing off, once all fifteen men have been brought into his homeboard. If one of his men is then hit by his opponent, sending that man to the bar, then the player may not continue bearing off until that man has been re-entered from the bar into his opponent's homeboard, and has moved all the way round the board back into his own home. Once home again, the player can then continue to bear off.

How to Bear Off
As we have seen, each point in the homeboard is numbered (theoretically that is, you will not actually find numbers marked on the board) from 1 to 6 inclusive and these numbers are of course equivalent to the numbers shown on the faces of the dice. When the player who is in the correct position to start bearing off rolls his dice, the numbers shown on the dice enable him to bear off one man from the point with the corresponding number. See Diagrams 288, 289, 290, 291, 292, and 293. He must not add the two numbers together for the purpose of bearing off, so that if he rolls 1 and 2, he cannot add them together to make 3 and then take one man off the 3-point. Each number must be used separately to bear off or to move within the homeboard, or

But if he plays like this then he bears off only one man

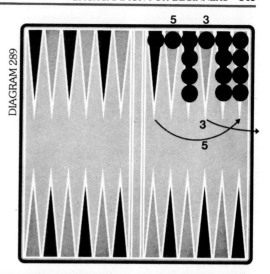

DIAGRAM 289

Again he bears off only one man

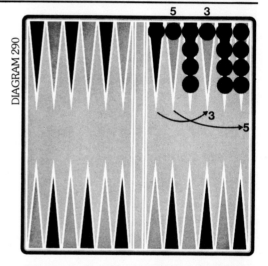

DIAGRAM 290

Playing like this, he bears off none!

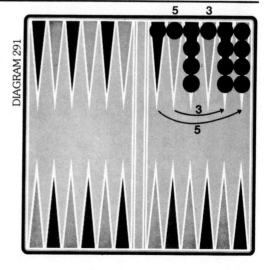

DIAGRAM 291

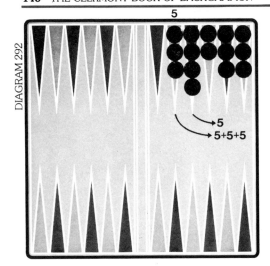

Black rolled (5–5); so he can bear off four men (the maximum)

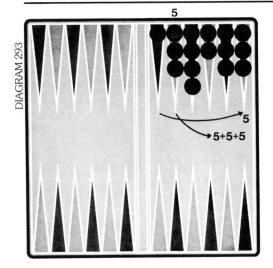

But like this he bears off only three

both when necessary and possible. If a doublet is rolled then, as mentioned before, the numbers on the dice (which are obviously the same) are used four times (i.e. twice each) so that four men may be borne off provided that there are four men on the corresponding point.

If the player rolls numbers that are higher than the number of the highest occupied point, then he must bear off a man from the nearest occupied point. For example, if a player rolls a 6 on one of the dice and no man remains on the 6-point, then he must take a man off the 5-point if one is there, or the 4-point if not – and so on, down to the first point until no men remain in the home-board. If there are no men on a point corresponding to the number on the dice but a man can move within the homeboard, then he must do so. For instance, if you roll a 6 and 5 and your 5-point is empty but you have two men on the 6-point, then one man can be borne off while the other man must be moved down to the 1-point. Whoever manages to bear off all his men first is the winner of that game.

The Start of the Game

To begin the game each player rolls one die from his dice cup (after shaking it) and rolls it into the right-hand side of the board. If the die is not void (in which case it must be rolled again) the player rolling the highest number makes his first move by using the number on his die and that on his opponent's die (as if he had rolled both in an ordinary move). If both players roll the same number they must roll again until one has rolled a higher number than the other. The dice must remain on the board until the move is completed, whereupon the player picking them up gives the signal to his opponent that his turn is over and the opponent may now play. Once the dice are picked up *you cannot change your move.* The opponent now rolls using both his dice, shaking them in his dice cup and rolling them on to his right-hand side of the board. After the opening move each player uses his own dice and dice cup throughout the game, each rolling alternately when it is his turn. The moves, as we have seen, are governed by the numbers on the dice, and each player moves his men from point to point in the manner described before, until the game is over.

Now that you have learnt the basic method of play you should study the rest of this book in the following order:

1. Sections 1 and 2 in Chapter I.
2. Chapter II.
3. Chapter III.
4. Chapter IV.
5. Sections 3, 4, and 5 in Chapter I.
6. Chapter V.
7. Sections 6 and 7 in Chapter I.
8. Chapter VI.
9. Chapter VII.
10. Section 8 in Chapter I.
11. Chapter VIII.
12. Section 9 in Chapter I.

If you study the book in this order the first time you will gain a thorough grounding in backgammon; later you can re-read any particular chapter in which you are especially interested – having first acquainted yourself with every aspect of the game as a whole.

PUBLISHERS' ACKNOWLEDGEMENTS

The publishers wish to express their gratitude to the following for the loan of equipment for cover photography:

Alfred Dunhill Limited

Turnbull & Asser Limited

Dormie Mens Wear (Hampstead)